Nonwhite
and
Woman

131 MICRO ESSAYS ON
BEING IN THE WORLD

EDITED BY DARIEN HSU GEE
AND CARLA CRUJIDO

Nonwhite and Woman

131 MICRO ESSAYS ON BEING IN THE WORLD

EDITED BY DARIEN HSU GEE AND CARLA CRUJIDO

woodhall press

Woodhall Press | Norwalk, CT

woodhall press

Woodhall Press, 81 Old Saugatuck Road, Norwalk, CT 06855
WoodhallPress.com

Cover art: Jing Jing Tsong
Layout artist: LJ Mucci

Library of Congress Cataloging-in-Publication Data available

ISBN 978-1-949116-69-4 (paper: alk paper)
ISBN 978-1-949116-70-0 (electronic)

First Edition

Distributed by Independent Publishers Group
(800) 888-4741

Printed in the United States of America

This is a work of creative nonfiction. All of the events in this collection are true to the best of the authors' memory. Some names and identifying features may have been changed to protect the identity of certain parties. The authors in no way represent any company, corporation, or brand, mentioned herein. The views expressed in this collection are solely those of the authors.

To the women who see themselves reflected in these pages.

Own your stories,
find a way to tell them,
and share them with the world.

won't you celebrate with me
what i have shaped into
a kind of life? i had no model.
born in babylon
both nonwhite and woman
what did i see to be except myself?
i made it up
here on this bridge between
starshine and clay,
my one hand holding tight
my other hand; come celebrate
with me that everyday
something has tried to kill me
and has failed.

—*Lucille Clifton*

CONTENTS

FORWARD

BY DR. CLAUDIA FEMENÍAS

When I began reading these micro essays, I found myself captivated as I compared my own experiences to the ones I was reading about. I remembered my own response when people changed my name, when I was constantly asked where I was really from, or when I was told I was not Chilean but Hispanic. Thus began an internal conversation between me and the authors, a dialogue where a diversity of voices and experiences found common ground while sharing their unique and individual stories.

Nonwhite and Woman creates a spaciousness for the voices of women from a wide spectrum of ethnicities and cultures to be heard. This anthology explores our commonalities, our differences, our life stories, and it couldn't come at a better time. Themes of family, mothers, daughters, grandmothers, food, language, the color of our skin, our bodies, and the use of silence, encourage us to reflect on what it means to be a nonwhite woman in this country. We are invisible and erased, we don't belong, we live between two cultures, we face violence, racism, and prejudice. Yet despite these harsh realities, there is joy. There is community. There is an overwhelming celebration of empowerment, pride, and connection. May you feel compelled to add your voice to the ones within these pages—I know I have.

Originally from Chile, Dr. Claudia Femenías lives in North Carolina. She is a professor of Spanish at High Point University and teaches in the Department of World Languages, Literatures and Cultures as well as the Women and Gender Studies Program with a particular focus on Latin American women writers. In addition to her academic work, Dr. Femenías is an active member of the community and serves as co-chair of Casa Azul of Greensboro, a nonprofit that promotes local Latino artists and culture in Greensboro.

INTRODUCTION

BY DARIEN HSU GEE - EXECUTIVE EDITOR

How do we tell the stories of our lives? How can we offer testimony as women of color making our way through this world?

In this collection of 131 remarkable micro essays, you'll serve as reader and witness to writers voicing their experiences and claiming their place in a world that, despite its beauty and capacity for surprise, is often bewildering, exasperating, and at times dangerous.

Women of color grapple with a sense of identity and belonging, of trying to make sense of who we are and how our cultural and/or ethnic heritage impacts our navigation through life. External judgments and snap assumptions can leave lasting scars—what we carry can transcend generations. It is not unusual to find ourselves existing in multiple worlds or leading multiple lives. We are chameleons, more for survival than by choice. Often, we find ourselves feeling alone.

But we are not alone. It is our hope you'll find company in these pages, that your own experience may be reflected here in some way, and that you are encouraged to tell your own story. Each of these micro essays are 300 words or less but are by no means light-weight—they'll linger long after you've read them. Lucille Clifton's luminous poem, "won't you celebrate with me," served as our beacon as this work came together. Throughout the entire process, we stayed open to introspection and inquiry, to unexpected interactions and imperfections. By sharing our stories, we choose to celebrate this life we get to call our own. Come join us.

Nonwhite and Woman

Name
LORALEE ABERCROMBIE

My name always seemed incongruous with the face I saw in the mirror. A German surname and a first name designed "to get you a job interview," as my mother would say.

In my early teens, when I was writing with glitter pens and dotting my "i's" with hearts, I remember practicing my own signature, meticulously repeating the loops in the "L" until they were flawless. Driven by a determination that ran deeper than vanity, perfecting that "L" meant I could claim ownership over this name, and shake the vague sense of "not-belonging" that seemed to affect every area of my life as a mixed-race girl in a predominantly white world.

I was jealous of anyone who had one of those multipurpose names that could change its outfit depending on the mood. My father told me he'd wanted to name me Jennifer. I imagined how nice it would be to introduce myself as "Jen" and to have the ability to instantly create an exclusive community by being known as "Jenny" only to a select few. Though when I looked at my face—my mother's eyes, my kinky hair—I didn't look like any Jenny I'd ever met before.

After I got married, my first name was replaced with "honey" and my surname was one that I'd enthusiastically chosen to accept. For months, I indulgently introduced myself as Mrs. Abercrombie, and luxuriated in the corny retail store jokes that inevitably followed, until I spoke to a woman I worked with in person for the first time instead of over the phone. "*You're* Abercrombie? I imagined you to be a tall blonde woman!" One comment and I was right back in my preteen bedroom, staring at a signature of a name that didn't suit.

Driving Soundtrack
Karina L. Agbisit

Sitting in my new-to-me car at the DMV for my driving test at the age of twenty-three, my hands grip the steering wheel, and I fight to steady the pace of my anxious breathing. With the car turned on but waiting in park, I turn the radio dial toward the lower-numbered channels, desperate for the music I know will calm me down.

As the *ranchera* music plays out through the speakers of my first car, my heart slows, and my breathing begins to return to normal. As the trumpets blare and the singer belts out his *grito*, I am reminded of the road trips my family would make from our small rural town into the city, the car speeding past the fields of onions and potatoes and lettuce my family labored in for generations. My father insisted on playing the music on road trips, even though he barely spoke Spanish and the rest of us spoke even less. It would not be until I was nearly an adult that I made it a point to learn the language of my father's family.

The driving test proctor knocks on the passenger door. I hurry to turn the music down, not out of shame or fear, but because I already know music is frowned on during the test. At least I still have my Ricky Martin concert tee on to comfort me during the next thirty minutes of controlled panic.

In the years to come, the music that I never appreciated as a child, the music reserved only for road trips and BBQs with extended family, will be the soundtrack of my driving, my entertainment in standstill traffic, and my comfort in dangerous driving conditions. It will always be the root reminding me of home.

The First Warm Day of the Year
María Alejandra Barrios

What does it mean to be an immigrant in a country that doesn't love you back? Sometimes, it means long TSA lines, border patrol agents that smell your coconut shampoo ("Oh, are you Colombian?"). Racist Uber drivers in Oklahoma who say things like, "Oh, I don't go to that part of town cuz there's too many blacks." Sometimes, it means being invited to a picnic to celebrate Eid. It means getting henna in your left palm on a beautiful Friday afternoon. Eating Luchis for the first time and drinking cheap champagne to celebrate the graduation of someone you just met. It means drinking out of plastic cups and turning your head with recognition when you hear "Oh, are you an immigrant too?" It means colorful dishes of chickpea curries, next to a cheese plate from Murray's, next to Takis. It means looking at the dusk, undusting the picnic blankets and making loose plans for dinner in Chinatown. It means running to the 14th Street station, dashing down the stairs, and while you're racing to catch the train, hearing on the platform someone singing an old well-known tune. A song of longing from home.

This Is Not a Rehearsal
Hala Alyan

The days blur together in self-quarantine. One evening, my husband and I curl on the couch and discuss the situation. *What good might come from this*, we ask. It is the question of the lucky, I know. The question of privilege. Of those with jobs easily made remote and health care and savings accounts. Even being able to philosophize about bright sides implies the luxury to catch one's breath. Implies some pockets of calm and quiet and reflection. I'm not an ER doctor. Or a mother of five in a refugee camp. We live in a two-family house. We have our leather couch. Our dog. Our backyard, which catches and releases the sun. We are merely lucky and grateful and afraid.

I'm not an optimist by nature. I'm inclined to distrust and catastrophize. I have a body that tends toward adrenalized, a mind that tends toward obsessive, and when I have too much free time, I spiral. It's strange that, in this time, I'd be looking for silver linings.

I'm about to finish my nineteenth day of self-quarantine. My parents flew in from Beirut hours before the travel ban was enacted. I have still not seen them. Every day, for at least a few hours, I feel a pressure akin to a brick mount in my chest. I've noticed it eases during meditation, which indicates anxiety. I live in Brooklyn, in the current epicenter of the outbreak, and every single morning I flinch when I look at the news. The air is sharp with anticipation and dread. We are here—we are told by the governor, by scientists—for a good, long while. We are to remain indoors with our tap water and canned goods. With our unease and traumas. Our sorrows. Our selves.

Still, I ask that question. *What good?*

exceptional
ANASTACIA-RENEÉ

it's amazing what they
expect from you

give them your life's
blood & memories
too—cry ally ally ally

& then decide

you are not the kamala harris	black
you are not the michelle obama	black
you are not the aunt jemima	black
you are not the sha-nae-nae	black
you are not the lupita nyong'o	black
you are not the waitress/barista	black
you are not the black porn written by white men	black
you are not the fresh dryer sheet commercial woman	
with white husband	black
you are not the oprah winfrey	black
you are not the play it safe	black
you are not nigga i will put my knee on you/kill you	
in a car/your apartment	black

you are just the
    regular
pieces of black
easily worn & taken off
easily picked through
        amazing

weightless
Anastacia-Reneé

don't ask me
what it's like
when you can't   imagine
the weight of the
world grown in my
uterus & you trying
to lift it
with robotic
arms
what i wouldn't give
to watch you lift
to watch you carry
this life of   black women
upon your head

How to Erase an Arab
Julie Hakim Azzam

"Israeli General Says Mission Is to Smash P.L.O. in Beirut"
Seventh grade, social studies—On the family tree, next to the names
of my father's family, I write locations of birth: Lebanon, Palestine,
Syria. I trace flags from my atlas. There is no Palestinian flag in the
book, but I know how to draw it. When the teacher walks around
the classroom commenting, all she says about mine is: "Palestine
isn't a country."

Palestine is a place where memories and stories are born. *Do I
remember Gaza or my grandmother's stories about Gaza?* Palestine is a
phantom limb that continues to send pain signals through the nerves.

"Car Bomb on West Beirut Street Leaves 25 Dead and 180 Injured"
Tenth grade, the foyer—Nicole steps into the foyer to pick me up
and is met by my father, who asks her if she knows what is going on
in Lebanon. She squints, trying not to appear stoned.

My father points a finger and yells about *typical Americans* and
ignorance and *privilege* and *nobody here notices.*

The day before, my uncle and his friends stood walking on
a West Beirut Street. A car bomb detonated and killed them all.
According to the *Times*, "most of the dead were unidentified."

When we get into her large, rust-colored Impala, Nicole snorts,
"The fuck was that?" No clue, I mumble, but I know that history is
a house I must live in. As the ignition cranks, I imagine it. Maybe
the men were talking about Amal or infighting among the Palestin-
ians. Perhaps over cigarettes, they commiserated over the mundane:
wives, kids gone stir-crazy, food shortages. They didn't notice the
unassuming Peugeot or Fiat.

Nobody ever does.

White-Haired Nana
Maroula Blades

This is my temple, a rotting shed beside a remote house up for sale, filled with dream catchers and spirited animals, torn out from pop-up books, now standing in shrines supported by rafters. Above the dark door, seven varnished shells hang that hold the whispers of an orphaned child who sought to hide her voice and loneliness in vermillion-colored eggs by a crepe colonial blue moon.

The only swarthy child in class caused her peers to squirm, turning tail to run if their teacher begged one of them to sit in the abandoned chair, reserved in the girl's mind for the visitation of white-haired Nana; her late grandma, who held the child's trembling fingers through a portal of light and drew closer to slap the solitude to ground.

Beyond the scratched desktop, Nana hummed her penned spiritual,

I'm beside you, weep no more,
there's light in the shadows,
weep no more, my child,

as paper bullets cut through air, fell to knot among cornrows. Pellets stung the collar line, etched a ring of plant-like bloodroots while eyes pinched tight in the scorching and ears folded.

Her silken tone rescued days when foul words whirled wounds with a whip the shade of the paper orb of night. Say-sos stapled themselves to memory where white-haired Nana soothes with incandescent light. She is not lost to the world and will never be.

Her spirit does not wane, but still flourishes anew every morning.

Consignment
Kimberly Blaeser

We spend our money unwisely. That's why we're poor. These words settle into the tapestry of the Ben Franklin basket, against beading thread my mom tossed in. She studied the print-end of each spool, like she was working out an equation. Cigarettes + thread = spaghetti supper. Her argument with herself is mumbled like those heard through Sheetrock walls.

"Shit!" She surprises me. We are always quiet downtown. Polite. Like when we attend a town wake. Even white heartbreak has a code. You tuck it into envelopes with green bills. You lace it into oxfords.

Here, before their glass cases, Mom only ever says, "Thank you." Her firecracker laugh disappears. Lips thinned, no eyebrow dance for emphasis, she pays from her green coin purse, clicks the silver clasp.

But today, words seep like steam from a pressure cooker. Then my giggles well up. I elbow her.

Maybe the teacher said, "Indians." *Indians spend their money unwisely.* The single sheet of black felt at the bottom of the basket seems to repeat this. "Fifteen cents," I retort. Silently, in my head.

My mom sews Barbie clothes and the fairytale couple at the Model Meat Market displays them. Today window Barbie wears a fawn-colored fringed jacket. Mom says my doll has to wait awhile until she can afford one. "Like on consignment?" I ask.

At Athmann's, we put money down on winter coats. My mom sends me with ten-dollar bills. The clerk subtracts; the line of figures snakes onto the back. Sometimes my dad sends extra money before October snow. I wear my coat in the house, hot in the furry hood. My mom takes a picture for Daddy in Billings.

I guess pictures are one way we are unwise. I never mention this. Instead, I smile like a Sears catalog girl.

Living Brave

KIMBERLY BLAESER

My activism was settled long ago. I tend to believe there must be some blood knowledge of past bloodlettings—a sensibility in some way inherited. But sometimes, I resist.

At a small-town T-ball practice, I am a kindergarten mother among male coaches. My ponytailed daughter huddles confidently with strong-armed little boys. Her baseball cap sits backwards, signaling her seriousness. I make notes—turn the glove, follow through.

For any parent, it is work enough to hold hope at each new venture that their child will measure up, be happy, fit in. Having weathered that heart work today, I am ready to gather glove, ball, and child, reward us with Dairy Queen, and head home. *WHAM!* That is the sound of fate whacking a reluctant activist *splat* on the back of her head.

I almost missed it. One minute we have our hands in, the coach is teaching us a team rhyme. We are almost finished, ready to cruise outta here, happy trails, the whole bit. Then I hear it. Did I really hear it? Oh no, no, no. This is my sabbatical year. I have just finished agonizing scholarly projects. I have volunteered in the school. For heaven's sake, I have done fundraising! I am finally about to unfold a deck chair and relax. After the hand toss, we leave, drive home, my daughter still high on camaraderie. I desperately want this duty not to fall to me.

After lamenting fate, coincidence, and my prickly conscience, I call the head coach. Fingers crossed, I ask if I heard the name correctly. Are we really "The Braves"? Yes, we are. He has coached the Braves ever since he started coaching. *Okay, well. Hmm.* My mind says, it's T-ball, Kim. So what? But my hands are already folding up the deck chair.

On Being Made Whole
ʻIolani Brosio

Parts of me were gathered by many hands
    weathered brown hands tattooed by time
    fresh, dark hands warm as pāhoehoe
    hands cool as a singing stream
    quiet hands as soft as kapa
    we wrap around the bones of our dead

Parts of me were deftly plucked
    like the prized feathers of chiefly birds
    from forests of the deepest black
    strands smoothed and oiled with kukui
    these anointed forests sprouting
    new parts of me as the years wore on

Before I became whole,
    parts of me were gathered
        in the finest of wooden bowls
        carved from the heart of an ancient one
    and there, parts of me waited
    as more parts of me were gathered
        over and over and over time

As parts of me waited, other parts of me traveled
    through currents of blue, ethereal song,
        and the slow moving depths
    these parts of me were called ashore,
        whispering with golden sands,
        gazing into skyward cliffs of the deepest green

Here, parts of me were gathered by salted hands
    that preserved our old ways

These parts of me were wrapped
    in the softest of kapa
    and passed to more hands
    hands that coaxed from me my secrets
    and in turn gave me
    my tongue of authority

These parts of me waited as parts of me were turned
    like the turning o ka iʻa o ka pō
    heated by wizened hands,
        those keepers of the old ways,
    entwined with my other parts
    tied together and fastened by mystery

So what is it to be loved but to be pieces gathered
    coaxed from the depths
    anointed by warm oil
    wrapped in the finest of kapa
    passed from hand to hand
    cradled near the hearts of the ancient ones,
    fashioned into the tongue of authority
                and to be made whole

Unearthing Joy

VIVIAN MARY CARROLL

Native children learn by example to be still and quiet when not at home. I learned from my mother. She treasured education. She named me after her favorite teacher and taught me to read and write. In 1954, when I eagerly climbed the steps of a yellow bus for my first day in kindergarten, I was unaware that nonwhite success caused resentment among the dominant population.

The only brown-skinned child in class, I discovered my joy for learning was not appreciated. Jealous eyes followed as I left class to study arithmetic in an upper grade. Muttered comments from classmates didn't stick. Degrading criticisms spat from the sour mouth of a bitter adult, the visiting art teacher, stung.

I had pet rabbits so I bubbled inside when handed a mimeographed Easter picture to color. I gave one rabbit brown spots, another was all black. The third rabbit, except for pink inside its ears, I left uncolored. "You didn't finish," the teacher said loudly. "Why can't you color like this?" She shook a boy's paper at me with green, red, and purple rabbits. I screamed inside my head, "My rabbit's white!"

Interpreting beats and rhythms with crayons while listening to Christmas music, my hand flowed with circles and squiggles. "You're just making marks," the art teacher huffed. Sinking into failure, I buried my art beneath angry red streaks.

Sixty years later, required to illustrate two stories for my BFA creative writing classes at the Institute of American Indian Arts, I hesitated, then splurged. I bought colored pencils, markers, watercolors, construction paper, embroidery floss, and glitter glue. Finally, finally, in a safe, nurturing, Native environment, I relearned the joy of art.

Mother Tongue
SAMANTHA CHAGOLLAN

She sewed the family together. Three-piece suits and flamenco dancing dresses and *Wizard of Oz* costumes, all without patterns. She could copy any garment just by looking at the seams of something similar.

Her opinions were plentiful and loudly expressed, on everything from the plotlines of her favorite telenovelas to the new sin vergüenza girlfriend your son brought home.

She refused to speak the language of this place. When her boys were younger and learning to speak English in their American elementary school, she tried to learn too. But they laughed at her mispronunciations and her thick accent.

She never spoke English again.

I didn't speak Spanish as a child, but on our Sunday visits I could understand what she was trying to say. She would cluck her tongue disapprovingly at the TV, or raise her eyebrows dramatically at the waiter when he splashed water on her napkin.

She didn't need to say much to be understood. Her words could be sharp, like the blades of her shears or the needles in her pincushion.

She and my father shared a vernacular. He could coax her to laugh, even when she was seething mad. When she asked questions she already knew the answers to, or slung insults around like confetti, he would call her out on it.

A thimble can protect the tender tips of fingers, but there is no shield from words that slice or prick.

She held on to her mother tongue, with pride. Whether her words stung or soothed, the clothes she made always fit us perfectly. Made with love for those in her bloodline.

Alien

VICTORIA CHO

My mother and aunt both received the double eyelid surgery. My mother, happy with hers, criticized my aunt's. *She looks like an alien.* Mom said I would receive the procedure when I was eighteen. She never asked if I wanted it. One in three women in South Korea receive cosmetic plastic surgery. In high school, when I wore makeup, I didn't know what to do with the eyeshadow because I do not have deep eyelids. I hated my eyes. My Asianness felt concentrated in this single feature that distinguished my appearance most from my white classmates. *It's all in the eyes.* I never left the house in high school without heavy mascara and eyeliner. My mother didn't mention the surgery again, and I didn't ask. I wanted different eyes, but I was afraid the surgery wouldn't make me look white—it would make me look alien.

Audition

VICTORIA CHO

At the advertising agency where I temped, a white man said he loved the agency's Asian women casting calls. He always visited those auditions. I sat in the office where he spoke, though he spoke as if I weren't there, or he spoke because I was there. A new, young temp in New York City on my own casting call. I wanted the role of making a life in New York City, but the audition was not going well. My five-hundred-dollar sublet with the air mattress on the floor and bank account balance of forty-one dollars made me suspect the city was about to close its door on me. I went to lunch and thought, *This is me now, I work in Midtown, I am in advertising.* Though I wasn't in advertising because I knew nothing about this industry, had no attachment to it, and was only there because the temp agency had no other jobs. I was a fake in an industry that emphasizes the fake in a part of the city with glass-paneled buildings and gilded storefronts and security guards. Silks and crystals draped on milky pale models, over their hollow frames and nippleless breasts and eyeless faces, but that man—that man said he wanted to be in a room full of women who looked like me.

The Color of My Skin

FELA CORTÉS

Imagine my surprise when I first learned that some people don't want to be Black.

In my parents' basement, I was surrounded by ladies whose velvet skin reminded me of the stunning women on the downy, blacklight posters. Handsome men with chiseled features and strong, earth-colored arms lifted my sister and I, placing us on the stairs to head up to sleep.

Even the waiters at the Chinese restaurant had haloes of soft curls and sported their Asian Afros proudly.

Our television rarely had any faces on it besides Gil Noble, Tony Brown, and Black academics and dramatists. We were only allowed to watch a few cartoons with people with paler skin, which was just fine, the Jackson Five and Tom & Jerry kept us laughing.

Our blackness came in a rainbow of shades—from the deep ebony skin of the most beautiful woman in the world, my mother, to the milky tea hue of her friend, to the gingerbread tint of our cousins. Black was everything.

Summers fueled our blackness to new heights. Amber tones sparkled and the Sun's rays brushed a claret wash over our faces. Black to the extreme.

During the summer following tenth grade, my world cracked apart.

In a rowboat on Central Park Lake, two of the girls who would become my best friends sat alongside me as we drank in the sun. Across the lake, two teens yelled, "Hey, you're going to get too Black!" The voices swirled in my ears. My friends, Korean American and Japanese American, rolled their eyes at the boys and kept chatting. And me? In the middle of the lake, I wondered how anyone could ever be *too* Black as I stared at the boys, whose ebony skin hid their thirst to be anything but Black.

Sugar Coated (1979)

CARLA CRUJIDO

She brings the caramel apple to school. Takes it out to the playground. Forbidden by the nuns, but she is a girl who doesn't abide rules. She invites herself to my house to play. I say yes. Don't know how to say no. She uses the bathroom. Does not flush. Her lack of manners astounds. Shocks.

We, at our private school overlooking the Pacific, are children of varying levels of privilege. Our fathers doctors, lawyers, engineers, owners of local beachside businesses. Our mothers, housewives. Moms. Our houses perch on palisades, rest blocks from the beach, sit steps from the ocean. One of us travels the world. Has grand adventures. One of us has a father who is the mayor. A manse with an ocean view. One of us lives by a former president. Wakes up to waves arguing with the sand outside her bedroom window.

I do not know where she lives. This girl with the dull brown curls. This girl with freckles that square dance across her nose. This girl who leaves shit in toilets.

The apple is too perfect to be homemade. She peels the wax paper from the drape of caramel. Takes a bite. Her gelding teeth leave a chasm of white flesh railroaded with brown. She passes the sticked-apple from girl to girl. Strands of blonde hair are tucked behind pearl-studded ears. Pulled into elastic bands. Bite. Chew. Giggle. Thank. She pulls the apple back. Looks at me. Asks, "You want some of this?" I nod. Smile. "Please," I say. "You got it," she says. Takes the sugar-streaked paper, smashes it into my face. Twists. The stick of it pins my eyelashes. My lips. Shellacs my cheekbones. The tip of my nose. "There you go," she says. Sniggers. Pauses. Then, "Mexican."

Are You Sure That Isn't Your Drinking Name?
Margarita Cruz

Margarita means daisy, I tell them. They ask if my parents drank when I was born—if they had always been alcoholics. They ask if the nurse wrote my name by mistake after my mom ordered a drink.

They tell me that a Margarita *sounds good about right now*. They tell me they could drink me up. They ask me if I am salt- or sugar-rimmed. They ask if I am good in bed—they clarify that they mean the drink and not my body. They ask me if they can buy me a shot of tequila. After all, I'm *not a true Margarita without tequila*. They pour it down my throat before I can tell them that I'm named after my grandmother, whose body is buried in Mexico. They order another shot.

They don't ask me if I like tequila. They begin to roll the r in my name and then they compete for the most rolled tongue. *Errrrrr.* They sound like bad machine guns in a telenovela, bullets breaking the night.

They ask where I am from. *Phoenix.* They ask *really* where am I from—what they really ask is where did the drink come from. I say *Dallas* but they laugh and tell me I am wrong. I do not tell them more. I do not tell them of my father and uncles who have never sipped a cocktail in their lives, who lived and grew up on the Gulf Coast of Mexico, who risked their lives to cross the border to give me this chance to stand here, at a bar where grown men who have only traveled as far as Rocky Point are telling me that I am wrong about a history that they never bothered to learn.

A Dagli for the Friend Who Emailed 10K Words—in Ascending [Dis]order—a One-Way Yelling Match of Why Trump Is God's Savior for "We the Sheeple" and Why I *Must* Agree

ELLA deCASTRO BARON

NAH.

That's all I can muster after years of trying. "I am unable to can," as Awesomely Luvvie sighs, so I'm not. A mantra: may my silence be a violence to your hangry ear and ego.

Just as snow has layers of whiteness, as privilege has layers of "rightness," I'll follow suit. This first layer of silence is me not replying. A mute mutiny.

The next is a barely audible sound (silent-adjacent?) of me bare-footing onto our front yard, inhaling air songs that smooth your slaughter-spiked soliloquy. The rat-tat-rattling, swishing leaves; the call and response caw and buzz and chirp. I ex-hurl my CO_2 waste toward the garbage truck beep bopping by.

The third layer of silence is me *still* not talking to you, but I sure am talking around you. For four-plus years with the Othered others, we've been over here standing in safe circles: peeling off the demoralizing layers of your MAGA word-votes as you try to tar and feather us. We detox, nourish, and massage the truth of *kapwa* back into each other's heart centers.

"You are worthy."

"I see myself in you."

"We are all connected."

I can *almost* enjoy these silences. Might even skip fists full of smooth rocks across your conspired catchphrases. Then, a barb confronts my skimming. You mention, "When you insist on being a POC, you cause division against me and other white people."

Save your slippery saliva. I'm nearly done chalking the white outline around our breathless friendship.

A Good Hike

Camille Dungy

Most of my life, my way of dealing with the feeling that my body was outsized or out of place has been to make sure I excel at whatever I ask my body to do. If I could hike as fast, climb with as much agility, ski as competently, paddle as aggressively as the folks around me, I assumed no one would think twice about the fact that a relatively big black girl was on the mountain, lake, or trail. Outside, people only care about size if it slows them down. I tried never to be the one to slow anyone down.

—

CAMILLE DUNGY is a widely renowned poet, editor, and author. Her collection of personal essays, *Guidebook to Relative Strangers*, was a finalist for the National Book Critics Circle Award. She has also authored four poetry collections, which have received numerous accolades. Her work has appeared in *Best American Poetry*, nearly thirty anthologies, and dozens of print and online venues. She has also been honored with two NAACP Image Award nominations, two Hurston/Wright Legacy Award nominations, and several poetry and prose fellowships. Dungy is currently an English professor at Colorado State. She lives there with her husband and child.

More than a Ghost

TINA EHSANIPOUR

To be Iranian in America is to be a ghost. I am constantly drifting, borrowing bodies, and never feeling like I'll have my own to claim.

But I do not haunt others.

Instead, I am haunted by the past—by a revolution that forced us to flee, by news clips of the Iran hostage crisis, by repressed memories of landlords refusing to rent to my immigrant family.

Perhaps it'd be easier to accept my place in this country will never be permanent. I will always be borrowing time and space. Always be expected to *go back*.

As a child, I would have been thrilled by the gift of invisibility, but as an adult I realize how exhausting it is to be unseen.

There are moments when I am allowed to emerge into the world with a body. But what am I supposed to feel—that this is only when there's an attack by a Middle Eastern man, or when my country is included in a travel ban?

I want to be studied, not as a supernatural phenomenon, but as a member of society. But not even the census cares to analyze the experience of my people, instead casting us into a pot to melt.

To be Iranian in America is to be a ghost of yourself. People have no problem consuming your kabobs and quoting Rumi, but they don't want to hear about generational trauma birthed from revolution. They don't want to hear how you simultaneously wonder about the life you left and worry you will continue to be othered in this place you have lived for decades—a ghost suspended between times and worlds that can never merge.

I want to be seen. Because I can't shatter walls if I'm invisible.

Pomegranates

TINA EHSANIPOUR

I used to love watching my grandmother roll pomegranates on the kitchen counter. Loved to hear the seeds crunching under her strong palms. Loved how this hard impenetrable fruit had a vulnerable side buried deep inside. Loved watching the red slip through as she stabbed an X carefully into its skin with the tip of a knife and pushed it hurriedly toward my mouth.

I'd pull the bitter, sweet juice into me, my teeth bloodstained, and feel like I had just drunk magic.

Maybe that's why I am the way I am.

Why I can't bring myself to package words into pretty phrases that are easier on sensitive ears. Discomfort is necessary to transformation.

Why I refuse to speak to my children in English, even in the company of those who don't speak Farsi. How else will their mother tongue find home in their mouths? Maybe that's why I am the way I am. Why I've never been good at hiding. I could have hidden in my pale skin, allowed white people to claim me as their own. I could have hidden in my easy-on-the-American-tongue first name, allowed the Iranian in me to assimilate. I could have hidden in the years I have called this country home, allowed myself to forget I was stitched somewhere else.

But pomegranates don't hide. We are meant to stain everything we touch.

30

Epistle from a Poppy to a Cactus

Dara Yen Elerath

I do not like you, truthfully. Your spines,
those small teeth, could tear me;
your jade ears are always listening. Your story
of survival is noble, of course, how little
you require, how you break the will
of wolves. Yet, at times I wonder—
would it kill you to be kind?
There are days I long for water,
for what you hide in your hard, green arms.
I have not the skill to coax you, to clear
your thorns. I yield to you, knowing little
of the sun encumbered plains you grow
so freely on, pushing your roots through rock-
riddled soil. I tally days I've spent
by you, days passed drowsing in this dry,
unsweetened heat. I must be tended
like other blooms: peonies, jasmine, those plants
any hand may gather, weave into wreaths—
those things that do not needle or force
attention, that plead for the affection
of insects, while you traffic with the majesty
of bats, of moths. Next to you I am small, standing
beneath the glowing mouth of the moon,
a reflection of awe at the parched and rim-rocked
ruin of this earth, this poverty that, between
the two of us, you the better have weathered.

How to Mount a Butterfly

Dara Yen Elerath

Be sure to hold her wings
between thumb and forefinger;
this will take practice.
Imagine tugging the unthreaded hairs
at the nape of a young girl's neck.
It is important to be swift
but firm, to brush her rouged cheek
with the back of your calloused hand.
When seducing a beautiful woman
insults make the best openers.
Mention mascara blackening
the rim of her lower eyelid,
or complain about the lace
fraying at the hem of her skirt,
the way she blinks too frequently
at neon lights that glow
through the bar's
smoke-darkened windows.
Place her in the relaxing jar.
Alcohol provides another way
to soften her resolve.
If a woman wears a satin dress
she wants you to imagine her
with golden orchids on her breasts;
of all flowers, orchids
are best at resembling insects
they want to attract.
Last, attach her body
to the mounting board
with a silver pin.
Lepidoptery is a hobby
often pursued by intelligent men.

Steam Iron

Dara Yen Elerath

When angered it is like an anvil. It flattens wrinkles on furrowed shirts, turns the topography of pleated skirts to level plains. It prefers deserts, earth battered into sheets of hammered gold. It is not soft like a washcloth or the cowl of a monk's cloak. See how it burns a hole in your favorite jeans? It blackens the seams and leaves its triangular brand—so like a rune, a hieroglyph, a cartouche—things deemed ancient, obsolete. The iron is resolute and cannot be swayed from its positions—dismal instrument, flameless furnace, silver bullet fired from no gun. Sometimes, you can hear the hum of a heart behind its metal plate. It pounds with hatred for any error: *I must crush muslin, poplin, felt, cotton; there must be no flaw.* Such are the thoughts of the iron. From the corner of its eye it spies a crease and feels it is in hell. *I must make it better*, it thinks, *I must get well*, but who will quell the iron's anxiety? Who will press it gently to cloth? Each night, the iron sings its only song: *something is broken, something is wrong.* One hears the tick of its expanding metal, the sound of something trying to settle—something crying, faltering, failing, and trying again.

33

Self-Portrait with No Flag
Safia Elhillo

i pledge allegiance to my
homies to my mother's
small & cool palms to
the gap between my brother's
two front teeth & to
my grandmother's good brown
hands good strong brown
hands gathering my bare feet
in her lap

i pledge allegiance to the
group text i pledge allegiance
to laughter & to all the boys
i have a crush on i pledge
allegiance to my spearmint plant
to my split ends to my grandfather's
brain & gray left eye

i come from two failed countries
& i give them back i pledge
allegiance to no land no border
cut by force to draw blood i pledge
allegiance to no government no
collection of white men carving up
the map with their pens

i choose the table at the waffle house
with all my loved ones crowded
into the booth i choose the shining
dark of our faces through a thin sheet

of smoke glowing dark of our faces
slick under layers of sweat i choose
the world we make with our living
refusing to be unmade by what surrounds
us i choose us gathered at the lakeside
the light glinting off the water & our
laughing teeth & along the living
dark of our hair & this is my only country

In Answer to Your Questions as You Pass Our Family on the Street

Theresa Falk

I am not the nanny. I don't charge for my services.

We are not a "blended" family. We're too loud to blend in anywhere.

Yes, they are both our children. It IS amazing how much my white son looks like his white father and how much my brown daughter looks like me.

They actually do look alike if you know them well enough. They make the exact same face when they don't get what they want: their lips curl up and they grit their teeth. It's more my face than my husband's, but indignation runs in our family.

She is a citizen, and so am I. My son is a citizen as well—oh, you didn't ask that question—

Yes, she is darker than I am. She is full Filipino and I am half white. How does that work? She's adopted. So is he. Yes. I am sure.

It is an incredible story, but it doesn't belong to you.

It belongs to us and to our ancestors: to a World War II nurse, a woman who made bombs, and a girl who hid in rice paddies from Japanese soldiers.

It belongs to immigration, an unhappy arranged marriage, San Francisco strawberry fields, and a pink 1961 Cadillac.

It belongs to a tender kiss in front of a coffee shop after a two a.m. shift.

It belongs to three birth mothers who changed their minds, and two who did not. It belongs to one lost son.

It belongs to the ping of an unexpected e-mail on Valentine's Day, to the beeping of monitors in a NICU, and to the white noise of an eleven-hour flight to Manila.

It belongs to heartbreak and joy and light.

Yes. We are a family. Why do you ask?

To My Daughter Reading Tolkien
Theresa Falk

Here is the thing I wish I could tell you: your mother is broken.

You probably already know.

At nine you are all longness and longing: legs and arms wrapped around themselves in a quiet, unknowing quest to keep your girlhood alive. Fingers tipped with chipped nail polish grasp book after book, turning pages to find answers to who you are and why you want to be. Do you slay the dragon or ride it? Do you dare to take its gold?

I stand watching you from the kitchen, wishing I could hold those hands with my own and tell you, definitively, to avoid the dragon altogether. That it would be infinitely safer to never enter the cave. That I have done so time after time and have been burned to a crisp, and that despite the strength I portray, despite the firmness in my voice as I tell you to put the book down and come to dinner, that sometimes all I feel I have to give you are shards of my hardened shell.

But I know I am wrong. Because you look up at me, put the book down, and in your eyes I see fire: flames that are not unlike my own. Take it back, I hear you say.

Take back the fire. It has not died, you say. It is only sleeping.

Let me awaken you again.

Eggs

ALISON FEUERWERKER

An egg is yellow on the inside, white on the outside.

I was born six decades ago in Boston. My birth certificate says, "Color: Yel." The Yel stands for yellow. I was not jaundiced. My skin was newborn-white-baby pink, a shade darker than if I had been an all-white baby. My mother fought to have the Yel removed. It is still there.

Wanting our family to fit in, my mother created new traditions for us that she thought were typical. Although we didn't celebrate Easter, one year we painstakingly dipped eggs into colored dye, packed them into baskets with green plastic grass, and delivered them to neighbors, including Ann, Sara, and Liz from my class. None of them became my friends.

An eggshell is brittle. Crack it and the insides spill out. "Your mother is a Ching-Chong Chinaman!" Holding up the corners of their eyes.

My mother protected the brittle white shell to keep us safe. As I grew up, I did not want that protection. The white surface of the shell meant I could "pass," so I dyed myself a multitude of colors. An Easter eggshell with the insides blown out. Hollow.

But being seen and known mattered. In Rwanda in 2015, a little boy peered at me through the window of the vehicle and said, "You are China." My heart cracked open.

In My Skin: An Autobiography

Fatimah Finney

(Age 8) She knew that the warmth of the sun, if felt long enough, could darken her skin. And she knew this was something to avoid. Prayer must be followed with action, so she didn't just pray for lighter skin. She sat in the basement after school hoping the chill of the cold, if felt long enough, could make her skin light. She was eight, and by that time she knew an unspoken rule. Dark is bad. Light is good. White is better.

(Age 16) She knew that having white skin was not an option and she was surrounded by what she couldn't have daily. A black girl on the white canvas of an all-girls prep school. The more she was around it, the more she despised it. Not the skin so much as the minds it cloaked. Minds intent on making her tongue, her dress, her existence the problem, though she knew her skin was the unspoken "intimidating" target.

(Age 24) She knew a guy who loved her skin more than she did. He wrote poems about it, planted kisses in it, and vowed to honor it for the rest of his life. His conviction of its perfection made her question the conclusions that she'd previously drawn. She'd built a love for her skin on the foundation of his. And when his foundation started to crack, she learned to be her own architect and took root in the stability of her faith.

(Age 32) I know my skin. Every mark, every tone, every inch. I see it with eyes that are more compassionate, a mind that is less critical, and a heart with more discernment. My skin was never the problem.

Cindian
CMarie Fuhrman

"Mama," I say. I am six, we are at Kmart. The costumes in 1978 came in boxes with windows that looked in on a plastic mask to cover the face which lay upon a neatly folded polyester garment to cover the body. "I want to be Tinker Bell."

"But you didn't even like *Peter Pan*," my mom replied, her hand holding mine, pulling me toward a dog costume, my passion second only to unicorns.

I pulled back. "Please?"

I imagined showing up to class wearing the fair skin, the yellow hair. My mom could tie my dark braids behind my head, and I would wear a white turtleneck beneath the yellow and green dress. Then, when Mrs. Sena led our kindergarten class around the lunchroom for our annual Halloween Parade, I would be indiscernible from the other kids.

For a day, none of my classmates would call me Cindian.

Cindyjawea

CMarie Fuhrman

My brother and his partner laugh and shake their heads. I have just told them the name I was given on a five-night canoe trip down the Smith River in Montana. We are having dinner at their apartment in DC where I have traveled to attend an Indian Education training. We are talking about Halloween, pejoratives, and an encounter I'd had months earlier with a local sheriff who insisted he knew *every Indian that's in Idaho County.*

"But you don't look like an Indian."

The three of us turn our attention to the man seated across the table from me.

"What does an Indian look like?" I ask.

"You know," he said. And begins to describe an outfit, a darkness of skin, two braids.

"You know how I know you're Indian?" I am seated across from a Picuris elder named Kelly. It is festival time in Nambe Pueblo. We are dipping fry bread in green chili.

"It's not your long braids," he continues, and I smile. "It's not your skin or some turquoise or beads you might wear."

I shift my weight on the bench, sensing the gravity of what he is about to say.

"I know you're Indian because you fight for Indians."

"Snow White," I say when my co-worker asks, "Well, who *will* you dress up as?"

"Snow White?" she repeats and looks at me, brows furrowed, as if trying to see the costume already on my body. "But you aren't . . ."

Dress Up Like an Indian
CMarie Fuhrman

"Why can't I dress up like an Indian woman? It's just a costume."

She was a student in my Native Literature course. We were talking about appropriation and she was set on proving that she had a right to dress up in the Pocahottie costume she'd purchased on Amazon.

"Dressing up and playing Indian is not a harmless activity," I said, reminding her and the other students what we had discussed after reading *The Round House* by Louise Erdrich. I recited again the statistics of sexual assault on Native women, one in three, and reminded the class that they are more than twice the national average. "A costume based on race or ethnicity extracts the human.

"And if those aren't enough reasons," I continued, "how about because it is unkind?"

"Unkind to who? All those Indians are dead."

A Tale I Have Never Lived
Helena Garcia

Stand up straight, kid! My grandmother ordered while marking my dress body measures. I needed to do a presentation with my class about princesses and their magic. I loved that utopia of a better reality, with perks and luxuries I would never experience. I was excited, rehearsing my performance speech in my head.

A few weeks later, the day came. I dressed as my favorite princess, Snow White. All the details were perfect, from the red tiara to the red cape and white neck dress. I felt majestic.

Every classmate looked incredible. I felt pride for them. After chatting with my friends, I rehearsed out loud. In the corridor, I started over and over. Then, a boy came. "Helena, you can't be Snow White. You're brown!"

I was no longer a princess. Every tale demands a villain. Racism has been mine. Even though I thought I looked like a princess, even felt like one, people's vision was different. That reality became worse every day.

I claim my heritage. I claim my curly hair, beautiful skin, and culture. Every tale necessitates a happy ending. This is mine.

Pull

ISABEL GARCIA-GONZALES

I dip my paddle into the water and pull, feeling wobbly at first, but as I get my bearings, my thoughts flow with each pull.

Pull. This isn't the open waters of the Pacific. It's an artificial lake in a filled-in quarry that smells of sulfur.

Pull. For millennia, my ancestors wayfinded by reading the stars and the movements of wind and water. I'm illiterate in this language, instead navigating my way through life using a map on my phone dictating each turn.

Pull. I wonder if our descendants will look back and marvel at how we had wayfinding devices that were also communication tools and knowledge repositories for our cultures.

Pull. I can't access the ancient ways of knowing and being. I'm just me, now, a Filipinx woman living in the unceded territory of the Kiikaapoi, Peoria, Kaskaskia, Bodéwadmiké, Myaamia, disconnected from my own ancestral lands, paddling a rented kayak on a summer day during a pandemic in the year 2020.

Pull. And isn't that a worthy, authentic life too?

Stop. I dig my paddle into the mud, anchoring the kayak next to the bird sanctuary, feeling kinship with these birds. They've made their home on an artificial island on an artificial lake in a suburban landscape of buildings not mountains, filled-in quarries not swamps and lakes, highways and malls not endless prairie. Does this make them any less bird? No, it makes them survivors.

Hold. A single white egret walks out on its long legs from the foliage, wades into the lake, hunting. The fact that it adapted to hunt in a fake lake doesn't make the hunting any less real. The egret looks up. We gaze at each other for a moment.

Pull. I begin to feel my place in the order of the Universe.

Persian vs. Iranian

GABRIELLE GHADERI

Technically, there's an ethnological distinction between Iranian and Persian, but between you and me, it's all the same. To-*may*-to. To-*mah*-to.

I used to tell people I was Persian for no reason other than it just sounds nicer. There's nothing threatening about a Persian. The word is soft like a fluffy white Persian cat. Elegant, like the ornate patterned Persian rugs. The word "Persian" has the scent of rose water and pistachios. It's sweet, like a sugar cube between your fingers right before you drop it into your steaming cup of tea.

But saying I was Persian confused people. "Persia doesn't exist anymore," they liked to tell me. So I settled for Iranian, instead.

But the word "Iranian" isn't so nice. Iranians don't belong here. Iranians are nuke-harboring terrorists. The enemy. The word smells like oil and open sewers. It's a buzzword for political debates. The word "Iranian" feels like desert sand blowing in your face.

Synonymous antonyms. One's a whisper, the other's a shout.

Part of the Problem
VICTORIA K. GONZALES

Caleb's latest gut-punch post reads: *Go back to Mexico.*
> He calls. "You on your way?"
> Rage slides at the edge of my tongue. I want to mention the post.
> Instead, I say, "Be right there."

In addition to his insensitive posts on deportation, immigration, and America being "great again," Caleb proudly sports MAGA attire, even after Milton was deported. Milton, an American name, light-skinned like me, green-eyed like Caleb, an undocumented immigrant. Our friend.
> Caleb's solution when he heard the news: "He should've become a citizen the *right* way."
> "What's the right way?" I'd asked.
> "Get a lawyer."
> "Then what?"
> He looked at me with empty eyes. "I know people who did it, *legally*, so he can do it, too, he just doesn't want to."
> I wanted to ask him, "Why wouldn't he want to?"
> I wanted to remind him how our best friend was called slurs, slapped with a label. A human being denied dreams and feelings. In defeat of his ignorance, I said nothing: to keep the peace, to keep our years of friendship intact.
> *Does silence make me a good person, or part of the problem?*

At Jay's Java, Caleb's car and Trump bumper sticker scream out like his post on my feed. I park in the empty lot beside him, overwhelmed with sensation. I spot his red jacket through the café windows, waiting in line. I sit in my car, thinking of Milton, my Aztec great-grandfather, and my strong Guatemalteco mothers, gathering courage, absorbing what little silence I have left.

46

The Cartography of My Face

MICHELLE GUERRERO HENRY

After Chris Abani

1.

"¿De dónde eres?"

Hands pulling hard on my dark brown curly hair, blow dryer screaming in my ear. "I was born here. Father's Cuban. Mother's Ecuadorian."

She shakes her head, accusing me of lying, repeating, "Tu no puedes ser hispana." The phrase lasts with each pull. Nervous I explain family history as if to justify my face. When I pay she tells me, "Tus facciones finas deben de ser del lado Cubano."

2.

"Why does your mother have blonde hair?" Elementary school gym class, sitting on the gym floor that leaves little plastic particles on stiff navy blue shorts, playing Duck Duck Goose. I think of summer vacation excitement, landing in a place that we want to claim as our own, the picture of my mother when she was Reina de Piñas. I giggle out, "She was born like that."

3.

Miami summers. Abuela holds my father's arms, looks up at him and asks, "Have you always been so prieto?"

"Si mami."

I'm not sure if it's annoyance or sadness that flashes across his deep olive skin, large bulbous nose, and thin lips. Think: Don Francisco. Later, he'll relish the sun's warmth, the nurturing memories of beaches he hasn't seen since childhood. Refusing to wear sunblock.

4.

Discomfort lodges in my chest, none of it clear. So we spit in vials, pull on veins carrying rich red blood, dream of women speaking Ladino, of offerings made to feet and trees, women dressed in white, my Cuban grandfather standing by a sea grape tree. I dream of becoming water, of ships, of swimming in the dark. *I travel around my body, land on large brown eyes framed by thick brown brows, full lips, an aquiline nose, and fall in love with the cartography of my face.*

Hair/Bhaal
SAMINA HADI-TABASSUM

The old vacuum cleaner was not picking up all of the hair so I began brooming the hardwood floors myself at night when everyone was asleep. I found coils of Yusef's golden brown hair in his bedroom, under the sofa and near the kitchen table, where he took his daily medication for leukemia. He was still a child and his hair had that soft flight as it landed into the dustpan. Then there was Najda's long, serpentine dark black hair that was mostly in her bedroom where she spent her high school days with the door closed, except at night. I remembered how thick her hair was as a child and the arguments we had each morning as I pressed coconut oil into its folds. Now she was a vegan and had stopped drinking milk and eating meat and her hair had begun falling like leaves on an autumn morning. We thought she became a vegan to make her parents angry because that is what adolescents do—just as I had smoked cigarettes as a teen to piss off my Indian parents. But your hair does not fall out if you smoke and your parents cannot always smell it on you if you wash your hands often and do your own laundry. Then there was my hair. I was the one making sure the children went to school on time, dressed for the day, washed themselves, and had lunches made before we headed out the door. My hair was brittle and gray, trapped in the dust, gliding gently into the dustpan, as if in mourning.

Passing in the Middle Kingdom
STEPHANIE HAN

I am unseen: black hair, brown eyes, a willful mute clocking centuries of emperor absurdities. Old men crush young, bludgeon sky that brings all to her breast. Factories slay lungs for trinkets. I claim neither kinship nor love. I descend from a provincial body that refused to kowtow. Battle imprints arrow through my blood. My mind shaped across the water by genocide and art. Cries that broke shackles. Hope finds harbor, but boats leave to sink. Far away, palm tree lyrics, ocean that turns knees to jelly. A Cosmopolitan is a sugary cocktail. Exile? A door slammed shut. Migrants flee to suffocate, refugees suckle the powder milk of dreams. Expatriates scribble bitterness for love and dollars. Tourist, a word for the lover of refrigerator magnets. Emigrant, immigrant, sojourner, traveler flip through a displaced thesaurus. Death, a final home.

Great Walls crumble. Cannibal rulers drive sleek cars, fatten prey in gulags, auction organs for copy handbags. Survival: a son, a cup of tea, a gold-plated toilet. I shut my ears to homeland tour poetry, read tomes on dumpling glories, fish dried in smog. The West spills seeds of belonging, but children cower in closets, weep behind smudged glasses, write of steamed rice comfort, the hurry-hurry of it all. Exodus. Swimmers ravaged by sharks, driftwood freedom. I bite my tongue; blood stains my shirt. In this village women long for sons, and rubber slippers cannot stop switches whipping the backs of calves. Bamboo scaffolds the blazing sun, boulders plead for space. This place gently buries us alive in memory's hole. I say nothing. Passing in the Middle Kingdom.

Elegy

IDA SOON-OK HART

Daddy lies buried beneath a blanket of unspoken words and unasked questions. I was twenty-six, too early, too soon to know anything. His pristine headstone vanished among thousands in a National Cemetery of overlooked Black heroes. I was lost in a maze of diagonal lines, blinding white in its symmetry, unlike the sloppy red slap of death.

As a teenager, I found a secret cache of photos deep in the cryptic recess of Daddy's drawer. Photos that belied the stories he told his American wife of me as a love child, born of a Korean prostitute. The frayed edges and cracked lines of the pictures exposed the times he tightly squeezed their memories. These were portraits of a woman loved, a child born, a sliver of family time together in the cordite smell of falling bombs. And finally, the smoke of lies told to keep his wife and familial peace. I stole his pictures and began to lie too. I became buried under the dirty warmth of white cocaine and cheap red wine. At thirty-eight, I rose from the grave and discovered words to speak and questions to ask.

I eventually found myself among burial mounds on a mountainside overlooking my childhood village of Sangok-dong, South Korea. Nestled below in the surreal green haze of trees was my former school building: the Sung Lim Mixed Blood Children's Institute. Further below, the public school I couldn't attend. I was teaching English in a country that had refused to educate me.

I did TV shows, newspaper articles, phone calls and letters, but couldn't find my mother. *Omani! Mother, I came back for you*, cried my heart. I felt her death in my soul as I hugged a mound. Graves keep their secrets; they give no answers. We live with unanswered questions.

Kkamdoongie in Korea, Kolored in Kentucky, A Chink in America

IDA SOON-OK HART

I was 6 when children in a Korean village refused to play with me, yelling kkamdoongie—darkie. At 8, I lived in segregation with my Black father; schoolyard bullies called me chink or Jap. By 9, I could read bathroom signs at Beech Bend Park in Kentucky, Colored Only, by an elephant stall with huge droppings. John Lewis and SNCC met in Mount Zion Baptist Church across the street. Congress passed the Civil Rights Act. When 11, Aunt Elise and I ate in the newly desegregated Iris Room, upstairs with white linen tablecloths and fresh flowers.

I was 19 attending a privileged college seeking to diversify. Overcoming panic attacks, I went to an Asian students' potluck. At 20, I marched against the Vietnam War in Washington, DC, awakened to the economics of racism and sexism. By 21, I protested against apartheid, listened to Angela Davis, ate only union lettuce, started a Third World Women's Collective. Black Korean in the Third World. Belonging.

I was 35, living in an underworld of addiction and homelessness, but nothing eased the loneliness of being "hapa." At 38, I returned to humanity sober, finding my soul again in teaching. By 39, I flew on American Airlines above the LA riots, seeing countless fires below. Rodney King. At 44, I worked in Seoul and felt my mother's oppression in a patriarchal Korean society.

I was 67, watching the killing of George Floyd, crying for all the racial murders of 400 slave years. Humanity marched in all the glorious colors of the world. Protests. Millions. Worldwide. Now 68, I quell fears of Asian hate to go grocery shopping. A neighbor asks, "Do you speak English?"

I am nonwhite. Woman. Hapa. Kkamdoongie. Colored. A Chink in America. Fighting and yearning to be seen as human within my lifetime.

Reader, I Hadn't Named It, Yet

Sadia Hassan

It is the first spring of a pandemic. I stop along a trail that snakes for forty-five miles across Northern Virginia to coo at viny plants I believe are strawberry buds. They are rounder and brighter than strawberries. Bumpier, too, with the same wide, jagged leaves crawling along the floor. I snap a pic on PictureThis, an app I use to identify plants. It turns out they are false strawberries, or snakeberries, not to be confused with the snakeberry plant, which is poisonous.

–

It is December 2014. I am in London for the first time and create an Instagram account to archive stories of images that are significant to me. My first post is of a Walmart parking lot. I miss "home" so much I bring it with me. The weeks whizz by and I connect with a friend I trust with my life. He takes advantage of me in a hotel room and I spend the rest of my trip denying the plausibility of assault.

–

The Internet is a portal. A book of beginnings. If I want, I can go all the way back to the day we met. A castle in Cardiff. A creative retreat. In memory, I do not care that trust is an impossible gamble, only that I am alive, unstained by the memory of a phantom after.

–

In the woods, I am the body encountering itself. White birch. Trout lily. Black gum. I do not trust a map or its markings. I watch the ground, listen for the weak wail of a goose trying to find its way home. My phone tells me everything has been named, that all the names have come through science.

–

At the heart of every story is a rape. I think about it in the forest, walking.

53

Greetings from the Land of Smiles

Lisa Lee Herrick

My finger is tracing the curve of the fabric on the pillow resting against the couch, the puffy edges of the elephant foot like two infinity signs intertwined, and feeling dimples of the cotton fabric puckering under my fingertips—the uneven exit wounds bereft of the hand that made them—and I am daydreaming and hearing my mother's voice humming me a song with no words, her invented lullaby for nights when there was not enough rice for seven and, now, she needs a distraction from the hunger chewing her intestines like bubble gum so she embroiders another pillow for the weekend flea market, her elbows groaning like starved trees in winter as the thread slips *shh-shh-shh* like a snake tunneling through the baked earth of the Central Valley, when I sigh that this pillow reminds me of my mother and that it feels almost like sympathy to find something Hmong in the world outside of that house I just escaped— the girl snaps, "It's Thai, as in, from Thailand, not whatever that was you said," but the words *noactuallythisisHmong* spurt from my lips, like a flinch, a reflex, a jerk; like an arm flexed immediately to shield the face from broken glass; and she sneers at me again, and says, "No, you're wrong, and I should know because I went to Chiang Mai last year and bought them there," and again my words spill out too eager, too urgent, a breathless wave *yesIknowbecause-mycousinslivethereandChiangMaiishometomanyHmongtourism-villageswhichisprobablyexactlywhereyouboughtthesepillows,* but she only stares at me, eyes half-mast and already bored of this strange girl her brother brought home last night who's now touching her pillows, and her upper lip flexes like I'm a bad smell. "Well, you've never been there, so what the hell do you know?"

Beige Mask #1
CHELSEA TAYRIEN HICKS

I ended my marriage and went to a concert in SF. I was a frontwoman, sang like a monster, poly. I wanted to know about what I wanted, not what the guy I was into wanted. There was a tall brown hottie in a flatbrim listening with concentration, unafraid to dance, hat reading, "PROTECTOR." His friend, also brown, complimented my dancing.

My steps were powwow.

"You should meet my friend! He's got the craziest name! Yellowhair!"

Yellowhair was my Flatbrim. I was into him. He struck me as a former Prom King.

"I *never* know what to say to you!" he said. He was high, gaping shiny white teeth at me, open-mouthed, over-expressive.

"Don't say a thing," I said.

I was trying to pass as Normcore Cool like him. Really I was an anarchist, a sad girl trying to pass as Happy. I didn't want to pass as White, but I could. I remember going to the Rappahannock rez when I was five, meeting the chief, a Native woman who looked like me. I wasn't confused. In the Independent, this rez-to-urban guy talked nonsense. He put his hands on me. We danced. I didn't know I was being addressed as a ghost.

Later, after leaving for Oklahoma and then Flatbrim bringing me back as Girlfriend, I was taking nudes of myself on his phone when I met the ghost. At first, I thought she was me. My boyfriend is the color of earth, a medium brown light for his tribe's colorism but dark for mine. He had broken up with this light-skinned girl to date another light-skinned girl from his own tribe. Cherokee Girl #1 wore a French manicure, two fingers extended around her pussy in the sigil of peace. I wondered if it was my skin that he wanted.

Beige Mask #2

CHELSEA TAYRIEN HICKS

Ahead of a modeling gig in Santa Fe, I left my Oklahoma reservation for Tulsa. Also, I had the private motive of waxing for a long-distance FaceTime lover in California.

The aesthetician looked Asian, I thought. She chatted in brittle politeness, asking about my job (tribal) and where I lived (my reservation).

She said, "Oh, do you have some Indian in you? I guess we all have a little something in us. I know a lot of Mexicans have Indigenous blood."

I didn't tell her I had misjudged her *groupa* too. I didn't tell her I felt like I should apologize for being Light.

"Yes," I said, my simulacrum of rude politesse. I didn't care to give her a talk about French intermixing, genocide, assimilation, and blood quantum policies. When I left the rez, it was like I was in another country. I went to my happy place, at Venice Beach with my lover, known by coworkers as haxe waleze gaxe nika wida. My Navajo man. *Haxe waleze gaxe wida.* My maker of striped blankets man.

"Would you like me to leave your eyebrows full, or?"

"Heavy Eyebrows is our word for White people," I said.

She did what I asked.

I left thinking how if we were in LA, we'd be dancing at La Cita together, not knowing the difference, not needing to divide ourselves like slices of butter. Here, in the Tulsa city salon, we felt the need to enact some type of violence. We played our roles, Light-Skinned Indigenous Woman #1 and #2. Our roles weren't even available in movies or television, but we did our best to make them up as they might've been, and to stick to the lines as they might've been, verbatim.

China Doll

CHRISTINE C. HSU

We were driven in a white Hummer limo to the hair salon.

My black hair was Texas hairspray high.
My lashes were long with ruby red lips.

My friend's mom gushed, "Oh, you look just like a China Doll."
I stopped.

Should I call my friend's mom a racist on her wedding day?

My blonde friend's mom was always good to me.
Bringing me along to the public pool, movie nights, and BBQ dinners.
Plus her parents paid for my bridesmaid dress and the whole expensive
wedding. I don't remember what I said next to her. But I do remember
not calling her out.

Should I have?

I still wonder if I did the right thing that day.

Lunch
KAITLYN HSU

Growing up, my mom was strict about food. Money was not an issue, but she had no intentions of sending me off to school to eat whatever "junk" the cafeteria served. As it was, that "junk" was what most kids ate, and, disgusting or not, I wanted to eat it too.

In middle school, I discovered vending machines and opted for the Cheetos and sour gummy worms everyone else snacked on. The trouble came when I would return home with a full container of jiǎozi (dumplings) or leftover hóngshāo niúròu (braised beef). My mom would ask me why I did not eat my lunch. I would lie and say, "My stomach wasn't feeling good" or "I wasn't very hungry" or "I didn't have enough time to eat." The excuses alternated, until one day she threatened to call the school and demand that the students have more time to eat. I stopped using the third excuse after that.

How was I supposed to tell her that I was embarrassed to open my lunch, let alone eat it? People said my food stunk. They said it looked weird. They would ask, "What is *that*?" and give my lunch a wary stare like it could grow legs and jump out at them. It did not matter if the food actually tasted good when they tried it. At the end of the day, it was different—I was different. I did not want to be recognized that way.

Yet.

Érase una Nariz Superlativa

Rogelia Lily Ibarra

Quevedo's poem has always fascinated me. Not for its density and high culture, or even the *chisme* that he supposedly wrote it to his poet nemeses, Gongora, to point a pure-blooded, inquisition finger at him, but because in some peculiar way I felt connected to the big-nosed cat in the poem. Sitting at a profile one time in front of my brother's computer, I see my dad and *tía* walk by. My dad stares lovingly, laughing he says: "Qué bonita y narizona estás mija." She adds that it didn't matter much since I was the last born, the *sobras*. The joke in my family: I had inherited my nose from the Talancons or the Gutiérrezes because it matched my uncle Narito's physiognomy. A passing observation and then it cut skin deep: never quite matched up to my mother and older sister's collected, tiny noses. Not the kind of *chatas* that the *norteño* ballads croon about. Those pretty, white-girl noses.

I did make it to Spain, studying abroad . . . damn, did I confuse the fuck out of the *catalanes*. Mystified by my cheap Mediterranean look and gringofied, *telenovela* Mexican Spanish. I could not tell them I was a *chicana*, so I settled on Mexican. That way they could fix me in their cultural consciousness while looking down on me from their noses. If I kept quiet and dressed the part, I almost belonged.

Real Mom

MEE OK ICARO

Until I decided to come to Korea, I hadn't realized how special the woman who adopted me was—how selfless, how enlightened. Most adoptive parents of her generation can't understand that searching for our origins isn't a direct affront to them. In truth, it has nothing to do with them at all.

Even with a childhood head injury and an inoperable brain tumor leaving her in a confused simplicity, there was something deeper my mother had always understood, something she never had to be taught, a goodness I was only just now coming to know.

Throughout my life, for as long as I had been her child, my mother had never expressed anything but admiration and sorrow for the faceless woman who birthed me, then surrendered me, wrapped in a blanket white as a flag. She always knew that I was her child, that the haunt of blood could never silence the bond of fate. That while I do not have her eyes, I carry their sadness; and with another nation's mouth, I laugh her great laugh. We know the same songs by heart. We finish each other's sentences. We've kept each other's secrets since I was old enough to tell lies.

I have spent these past weeks in Korea thanking her as I search for the woman who gave me life, knowing that the woman I have always called my mother has been hoping, more than anyone, that I will find her.

Hyper/in/visible
Amal Iman

To be Muslim in America is to be a warning sign—*Caution: Presumed terrorist approaching.*

Is to feel eyes on you at all times, even if you're in an empty room. Is to balance carefully on a tightrope, always one misstep from disaster. Is to never know the privilege of anonymity. Is to feel unsafe.

To be queer in America is to be a beacon of progress, because we have gay marriage, right?

Is to stand alone in the center of a crowded room, your reality the manifestation of everyone's worst nightmare. Is to be portrayed exclusively as white & male & gay & cis. Is to still be laughed at and kicked at and killed simply for existing.

To be queer and Muslim in America is to be rendered invisible.

Is to sit on the front cover of every brochure but in the back of every board meeting. Is to be eternally adrift, searching for sanctuary only to have "open" doors slammed in your face. Is to feel like a fraud because you can't be real if there's no proof that you exist.

R/evolution
AMAL IMAN

I wrap the rainbow-colored flag around my head, tucking the ends of it into the collar of my T-shirt. It's the last Sunday of June, and a crowd gathers past the metal barricades surrounding us, dressed in a colorful array of shorts, tank tops, and glitter. As I scan their nameless faces, I remember. The tears streaming down my mother's face as I come out to her. My father's calm face as he delivers words that erase me. "There's no such thing as gay Muslims."

Skyscrapers line Fifth Avenue, a familiar backdrop as I begin to march in the Pride Parade alongside my friends. People cheer as we pass by. I muster the courage to shout back, "Happy Pride!" I start to feel safe in my anonymity in a way I never could around my family. Here in this crowd, my conflicting identities become a celebration instead of a contradiction. Wearing the pride flag as a hijab is a public proclamation of being queer and Muslim, something I never thought I would be capable of years ago.

I am a revolution.

Women in the Fracklands
Toni Jensen

On Magpie Road, the ditch is shallow but full of tall grass. With one hand, the button-down man steers his truck closer to your car, and with the other, he waves the handgun. He continues talking, talking, talking. The waving gesture is casual, like hello, anyone home?

When the truck reverses, then swerves forward, as if to block you in, you take the ditch to the right. When the truck slams to a stop and begins to reverse at a slant, taking the whole road, you cross the road to the far ditch, which is shallow, like a small road made of grass, a road made for you, and you drive like that, on the green and yellow grass, until the truck has made its turn, is behind you. By then you can see the highway, and the truck is beside you on the dirt road, and the truck turns right, sharp across your path. So you brake then veer left. You veer out, onto the highway, fast, in the opposite direction.

Left is the direction to Williston. So you drive to Williston, and no one follows.

At a big-box store in Williston, a lot sign advertises overnight parking for RVs. You have heard about this, how girls are traded here. You had been heading here to see it, and now you're seeing it. Mostly, you're not seeing. You are in Williston for thirty-eight minutes, and you don't leave your car.

You spend those minutes driving around the question of violence, proximity, and approximation. How many close calls constitute a violence? How much brush can a body take before it becomes a violence, before it makes violence, or before it is remade—before it becomes something other than the body it was once, before it becomes a past-tense body?

Collector's Item

Alyssa Jocson Porter

My mother returned home with a Barbie—a Filipina one, adorned with a pearl necklace and bracelet set and wearing a maroon terno dress with oversized butterfly sleeves and a beaded, embroidered skirt. This Barbie was not available in the US and was part of a limited series designed specifically for Mattel's Philippine market in the mid-1990s. Before then, I had never had a doll whose face and skin matched my own, only a squad of pale blondes.

I took this brown Barbie out of her package, already planning to release her ponytail and brush out her dark curls, and to replace her elaborate gown with a floral bikini or a bedazzled denim jacket or a ballerina's tutu, to take her for a ride down the hallway in a white Ferrari convertible just her size.

My older sister admonished me before I could carry out these plans. "It's a collector's item," she said. Too precious for play. Maybe worth something someday. The doll belonged in its box, safe from my sticky, slippery fingers and my little girl imagination.

She was right—I would not own another doll that looked like this. Like me.

I bound the Filipina Barbie's waist with a twist-tie, anchoring her to the cardboard backdrop of palm trees, and slid her back into the pink box for safekeeping on a bookshelf.

Years later, I still look at her through the box's plastic window and wonder what it would've been like if I had given her a name.

Combative

ANITA JOHNSON

When the body fails, the spirit rises.

I forget the slow, searing, and painful death of being burned alive. I block the memories of passing out from the engulfing torture, inhaling fiery smoke that singes everything, including the hairs in my nose. I forget the pain and rage that hides beneath skin to manage the daily work of survival. Leaving you in fragments, barely conscious but seeking shards to make you whole except some pieces were stolen generations ago and the thief keeps changing clothes.

"Don't remember anything, huh?" The male nurse didn't bother to look at me. "You're in the hospital. We are giving you blood. Liver toxins went to your brain. You're in leg restraints because you were combative."

Combative? I'm an HR director.

Brown skin erases the human and triggers violence. Once, lost in the suburbs of Chicago, police lights flared. I had not run a light or driven too fast. We were terrified when he approached the car. My mom, sister, and I all had our hands up. No one moved. He asked for my license. In an even, slow voice I explained I was reaching over to get it.

Shining his light on everyone he chuckled, "Ladies, you don't need to have your hands up. You were driving slow—just checking on you."

"Yes, sir. No problem." Handing him my license, we sat still, silent, with our hands up. Mama grew up in Mississippi and raised us in Tennessee. Police lights faded; a collective sigh rose from the ashes of imprinted Black trauma.

Combative? A death sentence for brown skin.

Black Everything

TAYARI JONES

My first doll was a brown girl named Tamu who announced "I'm Black and I'm proud" when I pulled the string in the center of her back. As a baby, I teethed on board books featuring children explaining how much they loved eating vegetables and being Black. As a grade-schooler, I sat at my teacher's feet as she gave us a dramatic reading of *Philip Hall Likes Me, I Reckon Maybe*. I had no idea that there were Black children out in the world deprived of images of themselves. Keep in mind that this was Atlanta, Georgia, in the 1970s and 1980s. This was Chocolate City just after the civil rights movement. We had our Black mayor, Black school board president, Black police chief. As my father would say with satisfaction, "We have Black everything down here!" We were segregated, but prosperous. I understood that the United States was majority white in the same way that I understood that the Earth was 70 percent water. I knew it, but standing on dry land, I couldn't quite believe it.

Dear White Evangelicals
LEENA JUN

I grew up idolizing you. My adoptive grandparents—American missionaries with hearts of gold—saved my family from poverty and loved us as their own. Upon settling here, we attended a Korean church with paintings of a white Jesus in the sanctuary and hallways. All the Bible stories had fair-skinned angels with golden hair. At my grandparents' parties, you were sweetly welcoming, praising our culturally blended family. You prayed for us. With us. Over us. I grew up assuming you were God's ideal, even though as an immigrant, that meant I was painfully NOT. I tried to be the best version of you I could be, thinking you'd see my heartfelt efforts and embrace me as an equal. I was unprepared for reality when I became an adult. Suddenly I wasn't the cute little Oriental girl given a chance at a better life. For some of you, I was the promising young woman competing for the same jobs as your own precious offspring, and you started to back away. As I landed some of those jobs, you started to grow resentful. And now, as a fully integrated American citizen, you've thrown down the gauntlet. You still think Jesus was white and you still see yourself as the hero in every story. You demonstrate a haughty Christianity bereft of humility with the emptying of our churches now bearing evidence to that sad reality. You are happy to stand over us, but not with us, and certainly not for us. I want to thank you for your generosity in allowing me to live and work here, but I won't, because decades of enduring your self-righteous disregard is thanks enough. Sincerely, That Asian Girl.

Brown Baby

Kristiana Kahakauwila

My daughter, with her father's long legs. My daughter, with my mother's auburn hair. At birth, my daughter's skin is impossibly fair, as if she belonged to one of her grandmothers. At least she has that 'upepe nose, low and round like mine, like my dad's.

I wanted a brown baby. Is that wrong to say? My cousins and I were dark sturdy legs running into the sea. Kukui nuts glistening on the beach.

Is it pride to want to look who we are—as if who we are is in how we look? Is it protection, knowing that here, in Hawai'i, my daughter will have an easier time if she doesn't appear so . . . white? Is it somehow proof we're not disappearing, my dad and me and all of us kānaka, us Natives? I know I'm playing into color bullshit, into race and blood quantum, and all the ugly stuff I don't want to admit to thinking about. But oh, the satisfaction when, as she nears her first birthday, my daughter's skin tone deepens. As I recognize myself in her.

Stranger Danger

Kristiana Kahakauwila

I am grocery shopping at the local community co-op, hemmed by bins of quinoa and unsulfured fruit. In this Pacific Northwest town where winter's dark has kept us tucked into our coats, into ourselves, we've hit the first signs of spring: crocuses nudge their unfurled heads through patches of snow. I have lived in these northern climes for three years now, a transplant from Hawai'i.

A toddler wobbles toward me and points to the boxes lined in a display. I kneel to meet her. "Are these crackers yummy?" I ask, and she rests her hand on my knee. For a moment it is just her and me, that tender hand.

I am still years from becoming a mother. Years from returning to Hawai'i to raise my own daughter.

For now, I am still in winters marked by snow, and this girl who is not mine is smiling, reaching with sticky fingers for my eyeglasses, as children sometimes do, boundaries meaning little to them.

Her father swoops in from nowhere, finger pointing, and I rise to tell him I don't mind. Just smudges on the lens, easy to erase. When I realize he's pointing at me.

"Stranger danger! Stranger danger!"

He folds his daughter into his arms, shields her from my body. He smiles, almost with understanding. As if I will understand him.

"You have to teach them at some point," he says, and before walking away, points at me once more for clarity. "Stranger danger."

Voyager Dust

MOHJA KAHF

When they arrive in the new country,
voyagers carry it on their shoulders,
the dusting of the sky they left behind.
The woman on the bus in the downy sweater,
I could smell it in her clothes.
It was voyager's dust from China.
It lay in the foreign stitching of her placket.
It said: We will meet again in Beijing,
in Guangzhou. We will meet again.
My mother had voyager's dust in her scarves.
I imagine her a new student like this woman on the bus,
getting home, shaking out the clothes from her suitcase,
hanging up, one by one, the garments from the old country.
On washing day my mother would unroll her scarves.
She'd hold one end, my brother or I the other,
and we'd stretch the wet georgette and shake it out.
We'd dash, my brother or I, under the canopy,
its soft spray on our faces like the ash
of debris after the destruction of a city,
its citizen driven out across the earth.
We never knew
it was voyager dust. It said:
We will meet again in Damascus,
in Aleppo. We will meet again.
It was Syria in her scarves.
We never knew it.
Now it is on our shoulders too.

The First Time It Happened

BLAISE ALLYSEN KEARSLEY

He loved us right away. That nice man who greeted us in the rugs department at Bloomingdale's. My mother beamed and held my hand. She liked taking me shopping with her; salespeople cooed over me. It gave her a leg up for haggling and charming her way to a discount.

I was five. Shy but friendly. Peak cuteness. Little dresses. Wide brown eyes. Nappy, knotted hair always tucked into a black pouf of curls on top of my head. No one knew what to do with it.

I surveyed the low pyramids on the floor all around us. Stacks of neatly rolled carpets that smelled almost as good as the inside of a new car. I wondered if I could ask to walk on them. I'd pretend I was on the balance beam in gymnastics.

The affable salesman pressed his red tie to his belly with one hand, the other casually tucked in his pants pocket. He leaned down to speak to me, grinning with kind eyes. "Where are you from?"

I didn't know what he meant or how to place the *where.*

There was a moment of silence.

My mother said, "She's my daughter," and gave my hand three rapid squeezes. "Her father's Black."

The man shrugged and winked at me. "Well, you don't have to tell anyone about your dad."

His words sank into me. *But I love my dad.* My senses cracked open as a new nameless lesson was ushered in, one I could never unlearn, something I would never unfeel, a kind of innocence held for a ransom I could never come up with.

The man straightened up, still smiling, and turned to my mother. "So, what can I do for you today?"

What Do We Call It?

LENA KHALAF TUFFAHA

My first return to Palestine with children was in the summer of 2006. Israel's war on Lebanon had burned through July, while we were next door in Amman. The war loomed large and it was—as always—a madness with which we coexist because what else is possible? Nonetheless, "the situation," a catchall word used to describe the weather of protracted war, was stable enough for us to go to Ramallah and Turmusayya and Jerusalem, the places in Palestine we call home. And so we crossed the Allenby Bridge, and like many Palestinian Americans do, tried to enjoy the company of loved ones, indulge in late-night walks and too many servings of heavenly knafeh to count. We prayed in Jerusalem. We were stopped at checkpoints, our American passports ultimately granting us passage. In "In Northern Ireland They Called It 'The Troubles,' " Nye asks with understandable exasperation: "What do we call it? / The very endless nightmare? The toothache of tragedy? / I call it a life no one would choose."

At a checkpoint on the way from Turmusayya to Ramallah, a soldier—who looked to be twenty years old at most—smirked at my girls in the back seat of the van, flipped through the pages of our passports. My then-three-year-old fixed him with her hazel eyes. It was his machine gun she was staring at, as it dangled from his shoulder, brushing the edge of her seat. His slouch, the sneer, his delight in holding us there for a few minutes for no reason other than he could were all part of her Palestinian education. No one had ever spoken to her father the way that kid with the gun did.

A few days later we flew back to our home in the United States. Our safety is a privilege braided with the guilt of tax dollars spent—despite our voting and writing and activism—to pave the roads and build the settlements those young soldiers patrol. And in the Palestinian villages and cities throughout our homeland, girls like Janna Jihad are left with the unfathomable work of resistance and survival.

Hues of Mama

SABINA KHAN-IBARRA

Mama is a brilliant splash of pomegranate juice on white cloth.

When Mama went out with her bright clothes and saadar, she stood tall, not shying away from curious, hostile glances. Mama had long, thick black hair. Her partoog kamees were always crisp and she wore sandals to match.

When I was five, I wore elaborate dresses, parading around the house.

They look for ways to get the red stain out.

Once, in second grade, as she cleaned the caked blood out of my hair, Mama told me to stand up for myself and hit Brian back. I cringed. "No."

"Did your mom steal our drapes?" he had yelled. The kids laughed, even those I called friends.

I looked at Mama's bright pink saadar framing her beautiful face and decided not to tell her.

Maybe bleach would make her fade away.

When we went hiking, a young man asked how many goats Mama wanted in exchange for me. Mama cursed with words she told me never to use and said she would kill him in a voice that dripped with blood.

He dashed away, never looking back.

She gets more vibrant with each wash. "They call me terrorist," I said.

73

"Are you a terrorist?" She cut okra in perfect, uniform disks. "I don't know what that is." "Well, then. Who cares?" Mama handed over her knife. I cut the rest.

The tint is what she is known for.

When I was twelve, Mama made me partoog kamees to wear to school. I ended up in a fight because James called me a camel jockey. The principal was sympathetic.

I expected a lecture when I got home, but Mama asked me to pray and do my homework.

I look for pomegranates to color my world.

With my chin lifted, I sat tall.

Whose Skin Is My Skin?

Saheli Khastagir

Mother grinds almond and mixes it with milk and oats, squirts half a lime to curdle it, empties a capsule of vitamin E, and tops it with a spoonful of honey. I take the bowl from her kitchen to my brother's bathroom and apply its sweet grains on my face, my neck, the length of my arms, and wait for it to pull at the skin. The mirror in this bathroom has been bruised from years of being slapped with the iron of hard water that turns everything red, so that my face looks ethereal, emerging hazy but tube-light-lit from the dark cloud of my torso. When I come out freshly scrubbed, she traces my face with the pride of an artisan. Her daily administrations slowly fades away the layers of dark I have accumulated in that land of whiteness, removes the lines separating the different shades of brown from my face and limbs so that I am one continuous luminous flesh of beige. How do I tell her that it is these lines that pull at him, that he outlines them with his tongue and fingers which are not soft like hers but which have held this skin, with all its shades, marks, and growths, with a softness I never thought could be mine, and that he loves it more every time I unpeel a new layer of kink for him. I try to tell her that while the sun makes our skin browner, it burns and flakes and reddens theirs, and that they envy the resilience of our skin, the resilience that marks us with colors she now tries to erase from me. But I know this skin, like this house, was never mine to claim. Mother, lover, sun—I am un/made in the beam of their desire.

Touch: A Transcription

Amanda Mei Kim

My father's fingertips were shaped like dull piano hammers. Interlocked in his, my fingers were tender root shoots covered in dirt and grease. With a near-identical squeeze of his hand, he could either send me a message of support or issue a soft warning.

Whether it was my father's paw of a hand, a woman leading me down a grocery aisle, an unknown child pulling at my sweater, or a gentle shove when I was slow to board the bus, Asians and Asian Americans delight in the language of touch, and not because of any language barrier. A pinch or a kiss is more precise than a word, more urgent, more intimate, more honest.

I missed those touches during the pandemic—our shared currency of admonitions and affections. Instead, people pressed themselves against the walls when I entered the elevator, and worse, as I was walking my dog, a car swerved onto the sidewalk and two men leaned out to scream "TRUMP 2020!"

"ASSHOLES!" I screamed back.

I bought a taser soon after. My boyfriend Apollo bought a shotgun. We could feel the white rage that was overtaking the country.

The violence grew more specific, turning toward women, seniors, children, people collecting recyclables.

We had been dehumanized for so long, the laugh line to Jay Leno's jokes, that it was only a half-step to violence.

I told Apollo about the taboo that I felt when I saw an elder being hurt. "That old person is also somehow sacred to me." He held my hand. We didn't know what else to say. We knew how to relate as a woman and a man, but not as an Asian and a Black person, not yet.

Broad Margins
Eugenia Kim

After Maxine Hong Kingston

I didn't mind when they used to call me Madama Butterfly, China Doll, when I worked behind a bar. I was in my twenties, and I wore my Koreanness like a tight dress—it got me better tips.

My parents came over in 1948, and the latter half of six children were born in America. As if time were the quantifier of immigrant identity, being the sixth made me the most American of all. Except for food and household verbiage, I didn't speak Korean, and absorbed Koreanness merely through home life and Korean church.

When I got my MFA in literature and creative writing in 2001, I didn't want to be pigeonholed as a Korean American writer, though I was writing Korean American stories. All the lauded writers we studied were white and there were no teachers of color.

I had to research Korea for my first novel, and my parents' lives as well. The novel occurs in Japanese-occupied Korea, 1910–1945, and other than knowing that my mother had been imprisoned by the Japanese, I knew little about my nation of origin's history. I read more than two hundred books by and about Koreans and Korean Americans, and studied as much Korean history written in English that I could find. I pored through my parents' papers, took lessons in the Korean language—where the instructors were embarrassed, my being their elder—and in 2005 visited Korea for the first time.

Where once there was a vacuum of knowledge that I had avoided as being as other as I felt, the work gave me ownership and pride in the pigeonhole's broad margins as a Korean American woman, and showed me a place that had always been waiting for me.

jjimjilbang—bathhouse

Iris (Yi Youn) Kim

at the jjimjilbang,
i watch my mother's stomach swell and deflate
the flab of her paunch, the crevices of her abdominals
folding—in, out
her breasts, saggy and swollen with osmosis
dipping below the mineral water
i marvel at how my large bony 135 pounds of flesh
emerged from the bushy narrow orifice of her slight five-foot build
when i was a young girl
i used to be embarrassed of my mother's tendency towards nudity
the shameless way she strutted around
her unapologetic nakedness
as a woman,
i join her now in the heat and humidity of the bathhouse
surrounded by legions of chatty Korean women in the nude
immersing themselves in the communal springs and scrubbing themselves clean
learning to love my body is to love my mother's, in all its glory
to wash away the shame and violence
that i have inflicted upon my own.

The Path

KALEHUA KIM

I made my way in the world by being good. The dutiful daughter, the obedient child. Someone laid a path at my feet and I stepped onto it willingly. I didn't ask any questions, I kept my footfalls light. I didn't protest when the path closed in on me from all sides. I simply gathered up my skirt and kept my hands steady on the framework's walls, following what I assumed was a bright end. It was easy. It was uncomplicated. The frame kept me from wandering too far, from going too fast. I grew to need it. I kept my gait even and stayed always on the path. Surely what was outside was perilous. *The world is a dangerous place*, they said. My balance faltered if I took a hand off the wall. Any small noise echoed in that place, and so I learned to keep my thoughts quiet. I kept my eyes down because the glare was too bright. When the baby kicked inside my belly, I wondered what I had to offer her. I had nothing at my feet except this path. I had nothing in my hands except the dust from these walls. I raised my head and saw that the light did not reveal the path's end, but the bright flash of a train barreling toward me.

The Quirky Sidekick of Color Asks Her Book Club to Pick a Book

Kalehua Kim

I want a Happily Ever After story.

Help me find a story where the quirky sidekick of color convinces her friends to see the world from her place on the periphery. Where they see her skin, her people, her homeland, as rich and as vibrant as her biting wit that sends them into laughter.

You see, people can forget, even those people who are close to you. They can forget that their circles don't overlap yours in an equally satisfying and tidy Venn diagram, balanced in weight and power. Instead, their circles smother yours, inch closer and closer into your space so tightly that you don't have any way to breathe, let alone tell them to move over.

The quirky sidekick of color doesn't demand that you see *her*. She wants you to see what came before that *made* her. Her people were seen once, too, and they were beaten, robbed, raped. The heart she carries is a heart pumping the blood of her wounded ancestors. She carries it carefully, cradling it against her body. Every time she has to speak up or be seen, that heart grows heavier still. She knows that this is the only heart she will ever have, and that one day she must give it to her children. If you don't have to carry a heart like that, you can forget what it means to have your hands full.

So tell me this story ends well for them. Tell me her friends will work to understand what she's carrying. Tell me that one day they will lift her up so that she doesn't have to carry it alone.

When I Am Homesick

Kalehua Kim

My husband brings me mangoes. He lines them up on the counter, silently asking me to pick one. I choose the reddest one, with a blush of orange and yellow. Its smooth, tough skin comforts me, its heft feels right in my hand. I press it to my mouth and I can smell her. I smell my mother in the allure of her youth. I roll the mango over my face and we are cheek to cheek, my mother and me, heavy with the ripeness of memory. This is the first mother I knew, verdant and vibrant and firm. My palms tingle. I hold the mango in both hands, a heavy heart that I still carry because she asked me to. I press it to the center of my chest. *This is how I hold you now.*

Or Are You Normal

Lydia Kim

My parents survived the Korean War despite being children, marching and starving like adults. Now, they never test their luck. In America, I did not starve.

Today, I worry that I'm leading them to slaughter, walking them toward a new Asian market with a long line of people like us eager to get in. We wait between a wall and a parking lot, my hands touching the hollows of their so-small backs, ready to push them out of the way of danger.

Inside it's crowded with grandmothers and the savory viscera of home, a full array wrapped and glossy. Trotters boiled and sliced, plush sacs of pink roe, blood sausage dotted with rice. Like shooting fish in a barrel, I think, should a killer choose this place to be angry and armed.

I scan the throng for anyone who is not Asian and not shopping. My thumb worries the pepper spray in my pocket. I stay close to my parents.

I am not a mother, so I mother them. Push the cart and read labels aloud, reach up for the best trays of perilla leaves, heave bags of rice. Buy snacks for the ride back.

Were you the eldest daughter of an immigrant family, or are you normal, the joke asked, and its author gets her due, rueful, gentle agreement and animated mock-crying reactions.

I was. Sorted the mail, remembered appointments, answered the phone, answered for imaginary sins. I am. I make sure there's traction on the floors and bathtubs, ridged cups for their knobby fingers, blackout curtains for naps. No problems.

I am not a mother, so I take my vitamins, power-walk, stretch, flip mattresses by myself. See the doctor on schedule, save money, install a security system.

I have no eldest daughter, I think, with relief, and worry.

Currents

Yi Shun Lai

I'd like to paddle, like my friend Erik, down the Mississippi, through the undiscovered regions of this wonderful nation I call home. But the stakes feel too high for me. I can put my body at risk doing the things I love—mountain biking, rock climbing, snowshoeing. But these dangers are my choice. What tips the scale, moves the needle, is having that choice taken away from me.

What makes not getting to do an Erik canoe trip so heartbreaking is that, paddling through Minnesota, Iowa, Illinois, Wisconsin, Missouri, Tennessee, Arkansas, Mississippi, Louisiana, I'd want to dawdle with the wildlife, float in a couple of places, camp on whatever spit of beach I see. I'd want to talk to the locals, sample the local foods, read the local paper, get to know each little town on the river.

In some of these places, I'm not sure the towns would want to get to know me. In some of these places, I wouldn't be welcome. And while I have had good experiences in little towns, I've also had plenty of bad experiences, where the room chills, perceptibly, or goes quiet when I and my parents walk in, or where you just get stared at a little. Too. Long.

We Are Bridges

Cassandra Lane

I moved to California with thirty years of Louisiana in my blood—thirty years of its heat, its sheer heat, and the hairy mosquitoes that rise from swamp water to needle my skin with a steady intravenous drip of venom. I am at one with that climate's oppressiveness: my bones need marrow-deep heat, my skin expects humidity as thick as velvet. I have skin designed to take in the sun and hold it forever.

When we are from the country, when we are from down there, we carry star-studded black skies with us to cities whose skies are polluted by artificial light. We bring the creaking of floorboards, the thwack of splitting wood, the circus surround sound of cicadas and crickets. We bring unmarked graves decorated with plastic flowers the color of the candy necklaces we used to eat from around our moist necks. We bring the taste of our own skin's salt into our mouths and of just-slaughtered pigs, the gamey toughness of cooked coon and rabbit, the pop of BB guns. We bring the unsolved mysteries that live in the woods and in our own homes, the memory of our father's, papa's, uncle's, grandma's rifles. Gun control? We will remember that this means something else entirely to the Black southern family.

Physically, I left it all behind, but the South comes to me, over and over, in broken memories, in fleeting dreams and visions, especially when I am at my weakest, plagued by chronic fatigue. I am convinced this vague sickness is the residual venom of the creatures of my native land.

Girl as Map

Devi S. Laskar

I am not an island exchanged
for a few drops of turquoise the size
of a woman's tears.
         I am not your subject,
you are not my king. I refuse
to be the object of your fears
in your blue rectangle
world, a universe that holds a white bird
at its center. As for cautionary tale
for your ivory tower friends:
         I'm here
to stay, I'm more than dark myth.
I'm a legend, a subcontinent no longer
hidden. You cannot measure me in inches
or with a color-coded key.
         I'm scarred
sun, I bleed every evening as I set.
But I rise every morning no matter what.

I Words

DEVI S. LASKAR

These facts are not open to Interpretation: eleven years ago my home was raided by the Georgia state police, and my body was searched. Now, fear and anxiety accompany me like twin shadows. I'm no longer comfortable in my own skin.

Indigenous means native, local.
I am Indigenous to nothing in America except my parents' wishes and dreams. They Immigrated to the US before I was born, before I was even a possibility.
They landed in Northern California but moved to North Carolina to follow a better job opportunity. And so I am a Tar Heel by birth. But after armed agents raided my house in 2010, I fled my home and the South.

There's an I-word in GBI, the Georgia Bureau of Investigation.
But there was little or no Investigation, just Innuendo and the criminalization of office politics where my husband once worked.
In late 2016, a state judge in Georgia dismissed all of the charges. But to this day they have neither apologized nor returned my belongings.

I was a poet before my days as a journalist, and after, I left the world of newspapers. For a long time I chipped away at what was Integral to my writing life, trying to separate poetry from journalistic prose.
It took a teacher at a writing conference to give me permission to stop.
She too was a reporter once, and we have a friend in common.
She Instantly corrected my I-word: from Infect to Inform.
She gave me permission to journey from one side of the pond to the other, and have the waters mingle.
To illustrate my poetry with the news of the world.
To illustrate the news of the world with my poetry.

BUR to SJC: On Being an Only Child and Caregiving Road Warrior at 52

SHERILYN LEE

"When it comes down to it, it's about giving my parents the best day possible." #overheard

#876
Wake up at 6:10 a.m., brush teeth, wash face, change clothes, unpack my suitcase, pack small bag to take home. Clean Dad, take his vitals. Start bacon in toaster oven, low and slow. Sauté mushrooms and onions for omelet. Dad falls asleep. Collect trash, stock caregiving supplies. Put extra oranges in the kitchen fridge. Mom wakes up. Get on hands and knees to clean up ant invasion in laundry room. Watch alarm goes off—I have to leave for the airport in an hour. Go to Jack in the Box, pick up three orders of French fries for Dad and three egg rolls for Mom. The woman at the window calls me *mija*. Get back, make Dad's omelet, wash dishes, help Dad go to the bathroom, alarm goes off to leave, finish washing dishes, call Lyft.

#911
Today, my partner Grant and I met Lorna outside my parents' house. She brought us her homemade wontons and her friend's tamales. Mom made tempura. Dad enjoyed the food—he loves anything handmade, homemade. Lorna told us her mantra for the new year, "Just let all of it go."

#945
Being sick is not fun or easy for Dad. I distract myself with endless food prep and chores, but he is in a difficult place. It's been four years since he's been sick, since I have been home for more than five consecutive days. He did not feel well today and was very sad, the kind that's beyond tears. The kind that no one can do anything about.

But when I went to check on him today, he must have seen the worry on my face. He mustered up a little smile. Just for me.

Gray Matter

SHERILYN LEE

At home in LA, I write alone in silence—no music, no television, no phone, because my mind is distraction enough. Today and for most of the last four years, I have been trying to write while caregiving for my father in my parents' home 400 miles away where every moment is a distraction or an interruption.

This afternoon, Dad snores in his hospital bed in the living room, the big-screen television blaring, my parents' constant companion. I am trying to stay focused on the page. Dad wakes and raises his right arm, the one that still works. On the TV, Joe Cocker sings the Beatles' "With a Little Help from My Friends," asking the questions we ask in the spaces with our loved ones when we're vulnerable, uncertain, and afraid. I cap my pen and go to him as Cocker sways, grainy in the black, white, and all of the grays. He sings patiently, fully inhabiting the song. Dad sees me, his eyelids heavy, his mouth almost forming words. At his bedside, I smile and reach for his hand. Is he hungry, thirsty, uncomfortable, soiled? Words are no longer at his command; I search for clues in his facial expressions, a gesture. He's wearing his favorite maroon Henley. His hair is salt and pepper, his Korean Hawaiian skin smooth. We have not always gotten along. In my 52 years, he is the parent everyone says I look like, not my Japanese American mom. Sleep pulls at him—he looks like he did before he got sick, save the small curl on the left side of his bottom lip. His eyes close as he dives deep into the powerful mind trapped in his hemipelagic body. Where does he go? I wait.

Heat

LAVONNE LEONG

Whenever I text, *Will this pandemic never end*, my friend Paige texts back, *Breathe.*

Today, I am going to make *bo ssam,* tender Korean pork folded in lettuce with various sauces.

To be clear: it is Momofuku's *bo ssam*, a recipe I bookmarked last year, in the Before Times. Traditional *bo ssam* is boiled. This version gets slow-roasted then blasted with caramelizing heat, and its celebrity chef creator, David Chang, doesn't give a fuck whether you think it's authentic.

Last year, I knew nothing about making Asian food; I only knew how to eat it. Cooking it felt like a trap. You fold wontons for someone and he expects you to bring him his beer, forever. My Chinese *popo* didn't cook, except for party food. My feminist mother doesn't really cook, either. Our family heritage is to eat at restaurants.

Then I moved to a small town in Canada. It's friendly. It's also 5 percent visible minority, and if you want more than chop suey, you have to make it yourself.

Between then and now, I have apprenticed myself to black vinegar, ssamjang, the subtle uses of fish sauce. Red fermented doufu, star anise, dark and light soy. And sesame oil. So much sesame oil.

Momofuku *bo ssam* has hung out on my to-do list for a year. Who has a day to devote to making one dish? But it feels like giving up not to. Online reviewers described their families falling silent while eating, mesmerized by its goodness. I want to be mesmerized by goodness. Lately, I can never feel just one thing, be where I am, indivisible.

The oven comes to temperature. I rub the meat with salt and sugar, chop scallions, grate ginger. The kitchen fills with the smell of *bo ssam*, roasting. I inhale.

Amah
Selina Li Bi

She came from an island, oceans away, the Philippines. She visited us once. Her simple silk dress clung to her tiny frame. Silver gray strands among her dark wavy hair. Her feet, once bound as a little girl, hidden beneath red silk slippers embroidered with lotus flowers. She smelled of Pond's Skin Cream and herbs.

We had our own language, she and I—bobbing our heads, wild hand gestures like a game of charades. When we did come to an understanding, her face lit up like the flick of a match, her eyes a sea of gray-blue. *Hao. Hao.* Good. Good.

Mornings she stood by the stove, stirring thick rice porridge, adding slices of ginger root and scallions, filling our kitchen with sweet and sour smells. When I complained of a headache, she reached for the hexagonal jar of Tiger Balm, with its leaping tiger and gold-embossed cover. She'd dip her finger into the menthol-smelling ointment and rub it along my temples. I sat still, waiting for the throbbing in my head to end, waiting for the scintillating lights to dim. I'm not sure they ever did.

She returned to her homeland, but the memory of her never faded.

The day she passed, my mother received a call from overseas. Mother stayed upstairs in her bedroom all day. She was here and Amah was there, miles and miles away. I couldn't comfort my mother—I was too young. But I knew she yearned for one last touch. One last good-bye.

Amah appears in my dreams. A vision. I see her face, her eyes, her hands—those unspoken words, the bridge between two lands.

Postcard from Manila

SELINA LI BI

When we arrive, a brown-skinned girl places a garland of sampa-guita flowers around my neck. Its sweet fragrance is intoxicating, like perfume.

Mabuhay, she says in Tagalog. Welcome.

Coconut palms sway in the tropical winds. Beads of sweat trickle down my temples. The air here is different than at home, heavy and humid. At the airport, my family packs into a small van—me, my mother, my father, and three sisters. The driver looks at us and smiles, a cigarette clenched in his teeth. Enthusiastic relatives I only recognize from pictures surround the van and press their faces against the windows.

My youngest sister cries. She doesn't know they are family, too. She doesn't know this was once Mother and Father's home. Mother opens the window, lets the warm breeze brush against her face. She's smiling, bright like I've never seen before. Laughing. She turns and says *in Chinese*, "Are you hungry?"

I'm stunned. Has she forgotten who we are? Has she forgotten she doesn't speak to us in this language?

Our van weaves between packed buses and cars. A young boy at the street corner waves a packet of Marlboro cigarettes in the air. The driver honks the horn, swerves past a jeepney. The beaded rosary dangling from the rearview mirror swings like a pendulum.

Monsoon rains fall, flooding the streets. Our van floats like a canoe on a river. I lean out the window, my reflection bouncing off the dark water.

Call and Response
JOANNA MAILANI LIMA

When we next speak on the phone, my mostly deaf 83-year-old Irish mom will want to talk about anti-racism with me, her adopted Filipina daughter. I know this because yesterday in my mailbox was a cream-colored envelope bearing my name in her handwriting. From the uneven thickness I knew it was an article clipped from her local newspaper. Since I left home, this ritual has been a feature in our communication. Sometimes the articles are about travel destinations or random celebrities. This one is an op-ed about how Critical Race Theory is detrimental to American values and needs to be removed from public education to protect the truth of American history.

My mom doesn't know I've allowed a chasm to grow between us because two years ago, after I mentioned then-senator Kamala Harris and House Rep. AOC, she said, "Don't tell me you're calling yourself a woman of color these days." When she adopted me, my mom did not want to know anything about my biological parents, and she always claimed not to know my ethnic identity ("Skin color shouldn't matter"). My mom doesn't know that when I take her to medical appointments, the staff mistake me for her hired caregiver.

Even though I'd love to know how my mom reconciled with her alcoholic father after being estranged from him for ten years because he couldn't accept her marriage to a man who wasn't white, I don't know if she wants to hear how I bring social justice to my work as a therapist serving communities of color. From the sentences underlined and question marks in the margins, I can't tell if she wants to be an ally, or if she wants me to assuage her fear of erasure. Can we bridge this gap? Will I answer when she calls?

4(1)st Birthday Noodles

Joanna Mailani Lima

The ingredients are familiar: steamed fresh cabbage, carrots, celery; fragrant onion sizzling in oil; wheat noodles for long life boiling in salty shoyu and bouillon. Also familiar, the dish coalescing before me: the Filipino potluck staple *pancit*. I've never successfully made *pancit*. Today is a cooking lesson.

At the stove is my mother. She moves around my un-air-conditioned galley kitchen with ease, crushing garlic while explaining how she became interested in golf, spooning precisely chopped vegetables into the steamer as she laments travel plans canceled due to COVID. We stir chunks of chicken and laugh about binge-watching *Cobra Kai*.

Familiar. Familial. The intimacy of a mother feeding her child, the legacy of recipes passed from one generation to the next. Nothing remarkable about women preparing food together. Yet the scene unfolding in my home is miraculous.

Less than two weeks ago, I learned my mother's name when she reached out to me on Facebook to ask, could I possibly be the baby girl she relinquished in 1979? Now she's standing in my kitchen wearing jeans and a cheery yellow halter top and I'm thinking I should have offered her an apron. Surprisingly, she's a lot taller than I am and probably could have reached the white serving dish I retrieved using a stepladder. I felt too shy to ask.

When we reunited to celebrate my birthday together, my mother brought me a cake and a dream come true. When she discovered I wanted to learn to cook Filipino food, she offered to teach me.

> What uncut cords
> tether babies,
> mothers?

95

Behind the Mask

GRACE HWANG LYNCH

"When you ride the train to San Francisco, do you wear a mask?" my mother asks as we celebrate the beginning of the Year of the Rat over hot pot. Most people on the train work in high-tech; most everyone wears jeans, Allbirds, and down parkas. Hardly anyone wears a mask, except for a few Asians—usually very old or really fresh off the boat. That thin layer of paper and polypropylene carries so much weight. Once simply a barrier to germs used by doctors, the face mask has become synonymous with images from Asia: riders crammed onto a Tokyo subway or pedestrians shielding themselves from the brown skies of Beijing.

By mid-March, I'm not taking the train anymore. Offices, schools, and restaurants have shut down. But I can't hide at home forever. I need to buy groceries for my kids and husband, as well as my mother. My clothing for this outing is a sweatshirt from my kid's school sports team. Not just because I don't bother with nicer-looking clothes; with the panic spurred by account after account of my fellow Asian Americans being spit on, yelled at, and blamed for the pandemic, I just want to feed my family without being hassled. Can I signal that I belong in this neighborhood, this community, this nation?

The pandemic has brought once-hidden racism to the surface. But the virus doesn't discriminate: it will take up in any warm body, regardless of race, nationality, or language. In the Costco parking lot, I snap the elastic straps of the mask around my ears, steeling myself for the outside world.

My Home
Aretha Matt

My childhood eyes saw despair. I close my eyes today to remember my relatives. I can see their sunburnt faces, aging brown skin, and tattered clothing caused by days in the streets and the rancid smell of alcohol that settles into human bodies. I remember the defeated, emotionless, blank stares. They have lost their way. I grew up on a rural reservation adjacent to a border town where alcohol is sold daily to aunts, uncles, sisters, brothers, daughters, sons, mothers, fathers, and grandparents.

It was inevitable that as an adult I would decide to leave home for something better. A historical voyage at a university library gave me insight to my condition—rather, *our* condition as colonized people. Racist policies. It hurt me to read about the Native American children being rounded up by police. Babies taken from mothers to attend compulsory boarding schools where their indigenous values and practices were demolished. I was astonished by the Christian and White supremacist rhetoric that portrayed my ancestors as pagan, evil, and illegitimate, while their biblical teachings about love were buried under a deep-seated greed for the natural resources that lie beneath us. In time, we learned to blame ourselves and each other for the chaos in our homes and the failure to maintain our ceremonies, languages, and cultural practices.

Our narratives of survival are still swept under a racist carpet, while images of the Savage trapped in the past are broadcast. Mascots and people "honoring" us with "ceremonial" dances and tomahawk chops are the norm. We are made invisible by stereotypes.

I am a descendant of the Indigenous People of America. I have scars from historical trauma: genocide, holocaust, ethnocide, forced assimilation, removal from homelands, and urbanization movements meant to assimilate. This land is my home.

peril + power
DW McKinney

We met in our only-ness. One Asian. One Black. Both bristling in the hostile awareness of our cultural barrenness. Our conversations skipped from the coded language we spoke in our hushed office spaces and buzzed across the electronic waves dazzling the atmosphere. I cannot remember if I was drawn to you or you to me, but our kinship was inexorable.

We clattered with fury. Anger spewed from your mouth and your fingertips in uncontrollable rivers that gushed from sunrise to moonset. The contents of your mind gathered like a churning rage that frightened me. When I searched my own, I discovered the same distressing tides. History is littered with these familiar portents. Our forebearers once gathered in protest and, as such, the unflinching hatred of our skin has long been looped around our necks.

We healed in our togetherness. You and I, we emptied. It was a sorrowful sight, all that pain spilled across the universe. I cannot pinpoint when we shifted from brokenness to becoming a mosaic of hardened spirit. We shed the scales that failed us. We reclaimed the menacing fright of our heritage and harnessed our deprecation. We were warrior women, black and yellow.

One day we laughed in our freedom. And we have never stopped.

(un)Taming the Beast

SARAH E. McQUATE

When I was a kid my Black mother or my white father would braid my hair every night to keep my unruly mane of waves and ringlets from getting too hot on my neck.

It became a favorite bedtime ritual: me plopped on a pillow between someone's knees while they ran a brush through my wet hair, pulling out knots and then locking it up for the night. No more mischief.

Once, I left my hair in its braid for a week. It formed a giant dreadlock, and my mom almost had to chop it off.

In high school I discovered that if I sprayed half a bottle of detangler in my hair and brushed it into a ponytail, it would form a hard shell so that no frizzy hairs escaped. I thought that was tolerable.

The burgeoning chemist in me diluted the hair detangler—50 percent water, 50 percent detangler—and got the same result. Saved money too.

At one point, the hair detangler company changed their spray bottle nozzle. It misted instead of sprayed. I had to keep the last good nozzle and swap it out with each new bottle. I worried that I was going to get carpal tunnel in my finger.

In grad school I thought, *Wait.*

This doesn't have to be a burden, something I bind, throw over my shoulder and forget. This is my connection to my family—even now I ask my mom to brush my hair when I am home.

This is mine.

This is me.

I chopped it all off.

I left a small puff on my head and sent the rest to Locks of Love.

Sometimes I use conditioner.

Sometimes I don't use anything.

I think my hair likes this—it gets to be free.

Mean Well
CLAIRE MEUSCHKE

I see the ordinary man in the neighborhood who, for whatever reason, gives me intense déjà vu when we greet. Today, I'm not in the mood for the metaphysical. I linger at the hyacinths to appear unavailable.

Whenever I learned from a phone call that a loved one was addicted to this or that, I was the natural amount of shocked and not shocked.

One could see a woman looking at pictures of pink flowers in April and think *how lovely*. One would not see her frustrated search for the name of the pink flowers she saw.

I wear the shoes that cut into my heels, the weight of which make me feel hooved and carried by some herd force.

Some, if not most, of my childhood felt pleasant, which is what makes it all the harder to unlearn.

We would cross the bridge to our favorite uncle and aunt where we were fed mangoes. We learned to enjoy the green-yellow of unripe slices when placed in the same bowl in front of the same TV. We could taste the ripe possibility.

It is difficult to identify as a target when I felt so unseen in the first place. I identify as a late bloomer, but I knew some betrayals of body before I could speak.

So many on the perimeter wish for others to absolve those who hurt them, but mean well. I choose to never change. To never live enough to hurt anyone.

With a dull marker, I write on Popsicle sticks for the plant starts until the word looks spelled wrong

chrysanthemum chrysanthemum chrysanthemum chrysanthemum
chrysanthemum chrysanthemum chrysanthemum chrysanthemum
chrysanthemum chrysanthemum chrysanthemum chrysanthemum
chrysanthemum chrysanthemum chrysanthemum chrysanthemum

Life has felt too long already. Like I spoiled it.

Brown

DONNA MISCOLTA

In kindergarten, I discover I am brown. Or rather, what it means to be brown. Up and down the block of our Navy housing, white families occupy nearly all the units, except for the one next door to us. The family is Filipino. Like us, my father tells my sisters and me. Except not like us. We have a Mexican grandmother who speaks Spanish and makes her own tortillas and pounds seeds in a molcajete. My father speaks Tagalog with the neighbors, sounds that are mysterious and musical, and which belong not at all to my sisters and me.

The boy Canuto and I are in the same class. His mother calls him Cani, so I do too, but he becomes angry and says that's not his name. The other kids say Canoodo, which I know is wrong. I speak to him without saying his name, ask him if he wants to play. He ignores me.

After a while, he and his family move away, and a little girl and her parents move in. The girl shakes her halo of blonde hair in hello. When we play pretend, she is the princess. You can be the monster, she tells me.

Running While Asian

SANDY NAMGUNG

As a Korean American woman, running can be exhausting. Not because of the activity itself, but because of all the commentary I receive about my body and face. It's challenging to navigate running between these two cultures I identify with: in American culture, I'm invisible because Asian Americans are often underrepresented in the running community. Meanwhile, my face and body are hyper-visible and judged by unrealistic Korean beauty standards.

Growing up, I've always gotten comments about my appearance, but it wasn't until I started running that I realized just how widespread—and harmful—it really is. I fell in love with running in my mid-twenties and ran every day. People around me soon took notice. They started asking me questions like, *Why do you run so much? You're already skinny*, or *Aren't you worried about your legs getting big?* When I ran in the sun, I constantly received comments about how "dirty" my face looked being covered with freckles, or how dark my skin was getting.

I'm tired of people equating my worth to my face and body. The purpose of running isn't to make my body pleasing for other people to look at. I love running because it's just as much a test of mental strength as it is physically demanding. With every mile, I'm proving to myself just how strong, driven, and capable I am.

Haz 'ą́

SHAINA A. NEZ

Łigai 'go Haz 'ą́
"Color within the white space," I say to my three-year-old daughter.

Hailee is coloring a turkey. Her left hand holds the brown crayon with coordination, using her *'álátsoh, bee naalchidí, dóó 'álánééz* to work together. She spots the blank area and glides with the paraffin gently. At age two, her circular motions wild, scribbling past, unaware of the lines and rules. Her motor and cognitive skills complement her process—I continue to guide her. We glue cutouts of her handprints in colors *łitsxo, litso, dóó łichxíí'* for the turkey feathers. She eagerly moves and spreads her hand across the blank page for me to trace. At the end of it, she takes the pencil from me and traces my hand.

Łichxíí'go Haz 'ą́
It is two weeks before Thanksgiving. I wasn't scheduled this day with her but it's short-lived. 2020 is short-lived. We try to make the best of our days—creative projects, Head Start routines, and co-parenting. I stopped watching the news about COVID-19, death tolls, and Donald Trump. My days weren't to be spent in turmoil and mental devastation. I had to be whole for my daughter, who reads my energies well. If I sighed in a bit of frustration, whatever is in her hand she drops and walks away. I do my best creating the necessary spaces for her, our canon.

Dibélchí'í'go Haz 'ą́
My daughter will know the holiday's sham. *Asdzaan Tsóo éi Diné dóó bilagaana bilii.* Her spaces invaded on both fronts—her image reflects privilege while her thoughts battle oppression. "Brave," she says. She is not white—she is not #somethingelse. I discipline my thoughts and watch the brown crayon take up spaces. 2020 will soon come to a close; hope is not something for us to wait on.

To My Daughter's Future Bullies
Shaina A. Nez

I hope your parents read this to you aloud—we've had enough.

1. Please refrain from mocking my daughter's heritage in November. Do not ask if we live in tepees, as we are in the Southwest and geography isn't your strongest suit.
2. Do not judge or test my daughter's "Nativeness" just because she speaks better Navajo than you.
3. Bilingualism is real—that is Diné Bizaad she's speaking.
4. Blood quantum isn't a rite of passage—embrace your culture and language around you.
5. Next time, for show-and-tell, Auntie Chelsea can come by and show the children her regalia for pow wows. I'm joking; Auntie will come by and explain to the children how to act, because a dual identity is not nice to make fun of. Auntie Mariah is also on standby.
6. Yes, my daughter has privilege, but her mind is battling oppression—congratulations, our children still need extra guidance.

To My Daughter

I hope you keep this note, as a reminder of your strength, beauty, and competence.

1. Do not be your own bully—continue to love yourself.
2. You're no different than a full-blooded child, look at me; aren't you glad you have an English major for a mother?
3. Knowing your true self is far more rewarding than pleasing the outside world.
4. It's not you versus the community—it's you embracing your community. Always be proud of where you come from.

A Language Lost

Joan Obra

And then we were alone. Warm air weighed on my grandma as she sank into her chair. It's a good thing she didn't go on the tour of our coffee farm. The sun would have been too much for her.

She let go of her cane and motioned to the rice-winnowing basket. "I bought that bilao in the Philippines, Neneng," she said.

Unroasted coffee beans rested on its bamboo slats. We've been hand-sorting Hawaiian coffee on this bilao for years. "Yes, Nanay," I said. "I know."

Nanay and Neneng. Grandmother and granddaughter. When was the last time we'd been by ourselves, without relatives to translate? All seemed well as we chatted in Tagalog and English. The national and colonial languages of the Philippines, woven like bamboo in our bilao.

Nanay traced our family's path to the United States. First to arrive: my father, whose chemistry degree earned him a green card. Then my mother, who reunited with him months later. They brought over my grandparents. Then came my aunts, uncles, and cousins.

Suddenly, Nanay switched to Ilocano, my family's ancestral tongue. A river of words flowed from her mouth. I listened intently, jumping from one familiar word to the next. But the river surged, and soon I flailed amidst meaningless sounds.

"Sorry po, Nanay, pero hindi ko maintindihan," I said. "Can you tell me in English and Tagalog instead?"

Nanay smiled and shook her head. "It is very difficult for me, Neneng." She slid back into Ilocano.

In that moment, I envied my immigrant cousins. They'd arrived whole in this country, with fluency in English and two Philippine languages. But me? I'm the first in my family born in America. Straddling two cultures, I'm left with pieces of conversations, always longing to belong.

Manifesto for the Dreamland
Preeti Parikh

Henceforth, I decree:

▸ No wife, daughter, sister, or mother shall be the sole burden-bearer of virtue, the crown jewel of the family's honor. When I say burden, I mean *the* burden: the burden of being pure, being decorous, and the burden of always, always being good.

▸ Woman shall no more cart the load of honor on her head like some lissome belle carrying an earthen pot, brimming over with the water she filled from the river of her mother's womb and then walked back, balancing it along the dusty roads of her life's village; safeguarding in that fragile vessel, water that quenches her daughters' thirsts, water that one day will wash and purify her body, swathed in white, as it lays dead on a mud floor awaiting the soul's heavenly departure.

▸ From here on out, a girl's modesty is not a prize awarded to the most eligible suitor, not a treasure saved up and then donated in kanyadaan. Woman's purity was never tempered by the flames of a Jauhar or Sati; she did not come out of it cleansed, pure, forged like a perfect horseshoe.

▸ Set free woman's love from the ivory towers of selflessness and sacrifice; release her kindling from the timid fragrances of incense; let the flame of her engulf the world in its wake.

Daddy's Girl
Deesha Philyaw

"I got a new girlfriend" is how my father greets seven-year-old me when he picks me up for the weekend, when I slide into the front seat of his brand-new 1978 Monte Carlo, next to his withered body reeking of Champale and three-day-old socks. I have lost a tooth since he's last seen me, but his news of acquisition trumps mine. I like the girlfriends. Sometimes they have kids I can play with. Sometimes they have kids who are my siblings. In the absence of children, they dote on me.

"I got a new girlfriend," my father tells me, as if I care, as if I'm still seven, and not twenty, as if the new girlfriend is a woman a decade younger than him who he wants me to call "Mama Candy," who teaches me how to shuffle a deck of cards; or the tinkly-voiced, smell-good woman his own age he calls "Sexy Ida" like in the Ike and Tina Turner song, who always made sure I had a plate at the cookout.

When I tell my father I don't care, he brags, "Oh, but I got me a white girl."

A white girl, a not-me girl, got my father and his love. A love that lives between his legs, out of my reach.

The Exam

DEESHA PHILYAW

This morning, I tell my lover, "Ever since my mother died of cancer, I haven't kept up with my breast self-exams like I should. And I'm scared."

He sighs.

In a pamphlet buried in a box with my old diaphragm, these words: *Compared with their White counterparts, Black women have a lower incidence of breast cancer but a higher mortality rate of breast cancer.*

I am a Black woman. My mother is a . . . was a Black woman.

Tonight, when my lover and I are in the shower, I say, "I think I can do the exam now. With you here." And he sighs and says, "Okay." As I lift my arm overhead like the drawing in the pamphlet, the hot water cascades over my fingertips, trickles down my wrist, arm, and side. My lover, who'll become my husband, then my ex-husband, rests his still-dry hand atop mine, tagging along as I search for land mines the size and shape of a pea.

Move the pads of your fingers around your breast in a circular pattern, from the outside to the nipple.

The first woman he cheated with was Latina. He didn't know her specific origins, just that she wasn't Black, just that she was a dime bitch, according to the text he sent his best friend.

Feel for any lumps, thickening, or hardened knots.

I don't want to discover bad news alone. But my eventual ex-lover's hand is barely detectable, like he's already gone.

Feel that lump in your throat. Feel that hardening of his heart.

"I don't feel anything," I say, my mouth open wide, gaping like a hungry baby bird, letting the shower water drown my words.

Tell Us You're a Black Guy Who Only Dates White Girls Without Telling Us You Only Date White Girls

Deesha Philyaw

I like to travel, enjoy meeting all cultures.

<insert cropped photo of him with a disembodied white hand on his shoulder>

NO DRAMA.

<insert five pictures of him, the lone Black person, in group photos of camping trips and black-tie events>

I like learning about all cultures.

<insert cropped photo of him in profile, on the dance floor, clutching a disembodied white hand>

Must work out at least once a week and not let your body go to waist [sic]

<insert cropped photo of him in a tuxedo with a long lock of blonde hair tossed over his left shoulder>

Hoodrats need not apply.

<insert twelve photos of him with his biracial children>

I enjoy all cultures.

Everyone has preferences.

The Question
London Pinkney

Yet again we ask, *Who can love us like us?*

Redbone
London Pinkney

when i was first called REDBONE i was excited / probably because
it was something other than BLACK / probably because it was a
new thing / a new thing about myself / a new film a person can slide
over the projector of me / kaleidoscope my identity baby / free me
from my own responsibility / thank you for this gift / because baby
is confused / because baby is brown / ive never been BLACK my
whole life / my whole life i aint never been nothing but BLACK /
but i know you know we are all pink on the inside / like that dumbass
egg metaphor goes / were all crack eggs with yellow yolks / and we
are all from mother AFRICA / and we all have the same parents /
and boy i hope thats true / because if we all had the same parents /
id tell mother AFRICA on you

Misnomer
Saarika Rao

I am met with a long pause before an attempt at saying my name is made. A long silence usually means I am next in line or that I must make my presence known in class, something of that nature. I will sometimes start making my way to the front of the line or blurt out "I'm present" to spare whoever it is the trouble before I hear the attempt.

They say, "What language is your name?" I tell them it's Sanskrit, an ancient Hindu language. A language that reverberates through your dimly lit yoga studio when you are doing warrior pose and chanting "um" instead of "om."

They say, "How do you pronounce your name?" I tell them it sounds like the word "sari," traditional Indian women's clothing, followed by a few other letters, but I get the response, "Whatever, I'll just call you Sarah," or something that sounds more familiar.

My name, my identity, the root of my being replaceable, made more palatable, something to be shortened or overlooked for convenience.

A Seat at the Table
Saarika Rao

Sitting across the table from one another, condensation dancing down the side of my glass, I feign thirst while taking a sip to distract from the awkward silence and his unwavering stare.

After a few moments, which feel like a lifetime, he says, "You're pretty for an Indian girl," staring directly into my eyes.

A few weeks later, I am on another date sitting across from someone whose family is from the same city in India as mine, the first-time meeting in the dimly lit restaurant, the heat emanating from the fresh bread wrapped in cloth. I feign hunger and rip off a piece of bread and soak it in the small dish of olive oil to distract from the awkward silence and his unwavering stare.

After a few moments, which feel like an eternity, he says, "You're a lot for an Indian girl," staring directly into my eyes.

Pretty for, intense for, nice for, outspoken for, loud for, too much for, light-skinned for, dark-skinned for, too forward for.

Sitting at my mahogany dining table, I pull up a chair, pour myself a glass of red wine. My dogs swirl around my ankles begging for crumbs from my dinner.

I have a seat at the table. I am perfect for myself.

Track: "You're the One," by Fanny (1971)

BARBARA JANE REYES

Hell yeah, let this Brown Girl sing, because I know what I know and I know what I need.

I know there's no roadmap, no neat paved ways for someone like me.

I'm going anyway. Watch me go. I'm going to draw my own map. I'm going to lead me to myself.

I see some avenues, then everyone blocks my path, catcalling chickadee, cooing babydoll. They call me wild honey flower. They want to touch my hair.

Hell nah, I'm singing, hear me spin and weave lyrics with these woman hands, hangnails and all.

Hell yeah, let this Brown Girl be, ruby rock-and-roll gypsy in a big man's big dirty world.

I make ovaries of stone. I make the hottest blood. I'm the one. I'm my own thing.

Balancing Act

Roshni Riar

I did ballet as a kid, until the money dried up and we had to return my rented leotard and toss my ragged tights. I instantly forgot all the moves, but that didn't matter because I was good at staying on my toes. I was the only brown one there, but I didn't feel out of place in that studio, because I was doing what I knew best: learning to balance, holding my breath, shifting to find the perfect place to be. I was used to this on the playground, darting from my barely lingering accent, turning hard into Canadianisms that made me seem like, so totally white to nobody but me. When the bell rang, I'd glide home, omit the little truths about play fighting in the gravelly snow where I always miraculously ended up at the bottom of the dogpile despite being the tallest, and no, of course, I did not look at any boys, and yes, I will help you flip rotis and be the perfect little beti that you don't want, but now need. As an adult, I find myself constantly flexing my feet as I try to figure out which side of the barre I'm supposed to be on. The toes, they never find stillness. I realize, in conversations with white friends over watery beers, that I don't remember Christmases at my father's house because I'm not sure we ever had them. I recently retaught myself how to make chai, a recipe remembered from my grandmother. As I scalded the milk, the scent leapt back to me. I slowly relaxed my feet. Quietly touched my heels down to the floor.

By Blood

ROSHNI RIAR

I'm ten years old and have just awoken to find that I got my period while sleeping. Grandma is screaming, clawing at the spoiled fitted sheet covering my mattress. My pajamas stick to the inside of my thighs uncomfortably as I clench my legs together, trying not to look down at the crimson stain she is trembling over.

"This is ruined," she keeps repeating. Rage pulls at her features, morphing her face into one I've never seen before. "No one can ever see this."

At sixteen, Grandma and I are watching *Devdas*. Alzheimer's has stretched out inside her brain and made itself a nice, comfortable home. When she gets diagnosed, her guard is loosened by the devious disease. She tells me stories, how she fainted at the first sight of Grandpa, moments before their arranged engagement. I imagine a child scared of needles, going limp in their mother's arms at the doctor's office. Awaiting something they don't want but are told they must.

On screen, the camera pans into Devdas coughing blood into a white handkerchief. Grandma points, "It's like my wedding night." She loses her train of thought once the words leave her lips. Her observation clicks into place, bringing back that morning when I was ten. I don't remember how the movie ends.

When I am an adult, Mom tells me that the cultural tradition was to bury the stained sheet in family land. I wonder what they hoped would sprout from our blood, our duty.

My freshly shed blood was like a Rorschach test spread out on the ruined bedsheet before us. I saw a terrifying shove into womanhood in those drying outlines of blood, but Grandma didn't see anything, she felt it. The memory gripping the back of her neck, reminding her of what has always been expected.

Autobiography as a Panamanian Botanical Index

Karen Rigby

HIBISCUS	Fed on nothing like bonemeal or seaweed, but seasonal waters. Fire ants boiling in its jaw.
BEEF-STEAK HELICONIA	Among xylophone-flora, this was the measure for grotesque beauty. Raw, monochrome red.[1]
IXORA	Not Central American deer, though the name sounds otherwise. They're miniature globes girls divide into bracelets.
HOLY GHOST ORCHID	Petals fashion a dove encased in its own hood.
TORCH GINGER[2]	Garish runs in the bloodlines: Javanese florals like royal insignias.
CALLA	That everything named has been red or white speaks something about me that I can't name.
MAGNOLIA	In the white-rope hammock. In the house[3] with a lion's head for a door knocker. Let magnolia wind toward the zinc roof.[4]

---

[1] I was born in the capital. Omar Torrijos was president. Buses painted with saints flooded the city. Foil streamed from their side-view mirrors like sudden migrations.

Let me begin again. I was born where circuits nesting in the walls hummed yellow octaves. My mother named me for an actress at the drive-in theater. My namesake—traceless in the film vaults.

When I was born, a red drumbeat. An interior red fist.

[2] *Etlingera elatior* blends glamour with brass-band exuberance.

[3] Our neighborhood, El Dorado, lay one block from the Coca-Cola factory and a highway away from Gran Morrison, the bookstore emblazoned with a neon rose. The house was flanked by four palms; in the manner of citrus trees, each base was painted white.

[4] *Aguacero* does not translate. The closest word is "downpour." In Panama, rain funnels through the downspout for hours. It sounds like the beginning of the world.

Lunar Geography
Karen Rigby

Memory trails in the form of a postcard: the ink stamp recibido, a red and yellow mola, one more design in a background I've wished I could disappear in. I don't respond to my friend's postcard. I frame it beside a map studded with names I once memorized in school: Bocas del Toro, Darién, Veraguas, Coclé, Los Santos, Colón, Chiriquí, Panamá, Herrera, and La Comarca de San Blas. Nine provinces, one territory, something to count on each finger, a talisman that won't help nights I wonder why I once tried to erase my past as if a match had been struck. When I remember my childhood, I'm reminded of riding a train facing backwards. I know I will never return. Each day my memory blurs, until every image inside me brushes against the others like wind tearing through tall grass. I cannot see the beginning of the story. I cannot see everyone drifting like separate moons in the darkness.

Origin

KAREN RIGBY

In the wedding album my mother wears the same white dress she'd
worn for her high school graduation. She bares her teeth whenever
she smiles. It is 1974. My father's sideburns shine. Their arms link
as they pretend to drink from each other's champagne flutes for the
camera. They do not know their future. They do not know mixed
children can stare in the mirror for hours, wondering which side to
blame. Which side to thank.

Imperfect Mother
Rahna Reiko Rizzuto

As a young bride and mother, barely twenty when I was born, she wanted to see the world, but instead she found herself suffocating in the roles of mother, wife, sister, daughter. Our nuclear family moved to New England, where it got worse: There were many winter days when she gave up trying to leave the house entirely because as soon as she finally got three toddlers into their snow clothes, one of us would have to pee. She spent her days alone with us, and even ate with us alone because my father had to supervise the dining room at the boarding school where he taught. She tried, and failed, and kept trying to find herself; my father recounted a litany of her attempts: correspondence course, school plays, ceramics, weaving. I remember these: my mother's hobbies. I remember the floor loom she had when we were older, and the wall hangings woven with driftwood came to hang on every wall. The palm-size milk and sugar bowls she hand-pinched and glazed that I still have in my cupboard did not save her. Nothing helped, until we were finally all in school and she began writing for the local newspaper.

I have never been happier than I was when my father revealed that we depressed my mother and suffocated her. She was not the embodiment of the myth of the perfect mother I failed to be. In photographs new and old, people always comment on how alike my mother and I are, and now, more than ever, I can see the resemblance. She did the best she could, and if I could wish for more happiness for her in her early motherhood, she has shown me that you don't even have to like your children every minute to love them absolutely.

Just Like

ADRIENNE ROBILLARD

When we first moved to Fresno from Hawai'i, my mom joined the singles group at the Presbyterian church by Fresno State. After the Sunday service, a member of the congregation approached my mom and called her "Doctor." She explained that she's not a doctor. "Dentist, I mean," the man said. "I teach fourth grade," my mom said. There were two Chinese American women who attended that church in 1986. One was my mom. The other became our family's dentist.

I tried out for the soccer team my freshman year of high school. The coach was a tall white man, Mr. T. My mom and my brother often cheered on the sidelines of our games, braving the fog. Some of the other kids on the team told me that Coach T's kids were "just like" me, with an Asian mom. They were older and went to different schools. Their parents were married. We were not that alike at all.

My friend's mom seemed to want nothing more than for her daughters to have boyfriends and was excited that they had dates lined up for the Sadie Hawkins dance my freshman year. My friend's mom said, "You should ask J since you're the same. He's just like you." My friend defended me by stating that if I wanted to go to the dance, I would make my own decision. But that wasn't what bothered me. I didn't like being told who to ask to the dance because we were "the same." Instead of going to high school dances I hung out with friends at rock shows and wrote songs with them in my mom's garage.

Ramadan
Daleelah Saleh

"I remember back in March telling my friends at college how sad I was that I wouldn't be celebrating Ramadan at home this year," I confess to my mom as we set the table. She pours lentil soup into our bowls, while I fill small cups with *khoshaf*. She laughs, says, "Well, now you won't be spending it anywhere else."

"Yeah, be careful what you wish for," my brother chimes in, glancing at the clock. We're waiting for the Maghrib *adhan* to go off. It's 7:40 p.m. on April 24, 2020, over a month since I was sent home from college. I wonder how different this moment might be if I was back on campus, breaking fast in my dorm room or in the dining hall. After setting the table, I sit down and make *du'a* for what feels like ages. Finally, "Allahu Akbar" chimes from my phone.

We scarf down the dates, *khoshaf*, and soup, before heading to the bathroom to make *wudu*. We lay down our prayer mats in the living room and my brother begins reciting *Surah al-Fatiha*. After praying, we return to the kitchen and dive into the feast my mom and brother prepared, an array of classic Egyptian dishes: macaroni with béchamel sauce, stuffed artichoke, okra. Sirens blare in the distance, and I am reminded of how much grief I have been carrying.

But a sense of grounding washes over me, rooted in the thirst and hunger I've felt all day, and the relief I now feel after having broken my fast. Ramadan shifts my focus to abundance. A year later, there is so much I have lost, and yet I know there is so much to be grateful for. These two truths exist for me simultaneously.

Border Between

SHEI SANCHEZ

We drive up to the gate, leave the Jersey Parkway's Saturday afternoon croon, slow the city pace pumping in our bodies. My fingertips twist hush to my '90s mix. Eddie Vedder, a soft howl in the engine. Ma's fingers loosen their grip around the wheel, the office week behind her. Windows slide halfway down. I see spare spots on the glass, a display of just enough. Then, Ma's big smile cracks for her adopted world of over three decades: *We're here for the Bakers.* My head angles forward from the passenger side, bearing a smaller smile for a different world. The gate guard's confused, his face etching the edges of silence. Should I say something? That we're visiting? That we're not lost? I'm back for my own visit to this country, to my immigrants' America, after I left it two years ago to live across an ocean, to venture into a sea of other cultures. Then he opens his mouth, the sea spilling: *Are you here to clean their house?* Silence splits open, the ocean wave drowning our worlds. But Ma, with that smile draining the salt water: *Oh no, no. We're family.* For ten seconds, the border between us lifts, as if to say, "Welcome to our gated community." I look back at the white guard at his job. I look at Ma's face. Then mine in the side-view mirror. Then at the spots on the glass.

Not Safe for Work

MISTY-LYNN SANICO

They come on work-vacations as a reward for their performance and every year there is at least one: wealthy, self-important, "well-traveled," knowledgeable about everything Hawai'i because they once owned a vacation home here.

The orientation and management of visiting executives falls under miscellaneous duties as assigned. "Aloha, I will be your liaison during your detail for the next month," I say under a mountain of kukui nut lei and welcome baskets. "Welcome to the Honolulu office. I'm happy to help with anything you need."

These men take liberties and presume too much. They fill up empty spaces with opinions and the sound of their voices.

"You have such a pleasing complexion. Not so dark. Are you native?"

"Excuse me?"

"A native—you know, indigenous?"

I want to shout, "I am *Kānaka Maoli*. I am *ka pua a Līhu'e*, a child of O'ahu. Daughter of stormy Palolo Valley and the rolling 'Ewa Plains, baptized by rains, blessed by winds. I am sand and bone. I am *lā'ī* and *'ilima*, *kupukupu* fern and the *koki'o* flowers that my father picks every morning to adorn my hair. I am these things and more."

Instead:

"If you're asking whether I am of Native Hawaiian descent? Then, yes."

"You speak very well though, so intelligent and charming."

I want to stomp my feet, pound my thighs, gnash my teeth, stick out my tongue, and growl.

"Just adorable. You know, my son would love you. How fun would it be to have an exotic daughter-in-law. My friends would get such a kick if I brought you home!"

"I'd be a hostile souvenir but I'm happy to recommend items more appropriate for a man of your caliber and class. How about a set of shot glasses, or a bottle opener in the shape of a flip-flop?"

Korean Culture Camp
Misty Shock Rule

When I was thirteen, I went to a camp that taught Korean culture. My parents decided I needed it since I was adopted from Korea. I spent the week wondering, "Why am I here?"

I had no interest in being Korean. I didn't feel different from anyone else.

Sure, my sixth-grade best friend asked if my birth mother sold me. Usually I met questions and stares with a blank look—this time I burst into tears. But sobs dissolved into giggles when a giant snot bomb shot out my nose, my disgusting body bridging the rupture. My friend and I were laughing together, again.

In high school, I was the self-deprecating Asian friend. I made math jokes and put on mock accents. But I didn't know how to get in on the fun when my friends pointed at me, cackling about how flat my face was.

Years later, I'm the mother of a five-year-old girl. A friend tells me about a Korean culture camp for children of adoptees. I thought, "Why not?" and signed up my daughter.

She learns words, sings songs, and plays games Korean children play. One evening, she dances around the room while on the phone with my in-laws, chirping, *bisjalu bisjalu*—Korean for broom, her new favorite word.

"Go back where you came from," says my father-in-law, joking about something President Trump said.

"Not funny," I blurt out, mild words but the first scream of protest for me. It's time to start speaking up.

Now she's seven. I don't know much about our heritage, but I buy a kit with flash cards and a CD for learning Korean. One night, she bounces onto my lap, throws her arms around me, and exclaims "Umma," the word for mom.

We'll learn about being Korean, together.

Mother

SJ SINDU

My mother tells me to be careful. I'm twelve. We live in an apartment complex outside of Boston. I walk to school every day, a two-mile stroll along a busy road, and my mother tells me to be careful. What she means is, keep your head down, keep walking, don't talk to anyone.

I'm fifteen and my adolescent terrified-rabbit face is shifting into something that draws glances from older men. My mother sees them and tells me to be careful. What she means is, the world is cruel to women, watch your back, watch your back.

I'm twenty and in love with a woman. My mother is silent on the phone, then tells me it's a phase, don't I know what happens in the girls-only schools back home in Sri Lanka? She tells me to be careful. What she means is, this isn't real love.

At twenty-seven I date an older white man, and my mother is happy. Better a man than a woman. Better cis than trans. Better straight than queer. Better older than younger. Better white than black. She tells me to be careful. What she means is, don't get pregnant.

At thirty I'm married, and my ovaries grow cysts that burst in sharp pain. I take hormones to control them, and my partner and I decide never to have kids. My mother tells me to be careful. What she means is, too many hormones could damage her grandchildren.

At fifty-nine my mother falls down the stairs and dislocates her shoulder. She needs surgery, physical therapy, two years of healing. I tell her to be careful. What I mean is, I can't understand the fragility of your body. What I mean is, will I become soft and breakable too? What I mean is, don't leave me.

Mocha

GABRIELLE SMITH

Being Black is like breathing. I can't fathom being anything else. Hours of sitting on the floor, my mother putting seventy-something box braids in my hair. The intoxicating scent—Just for Me and Soft & Precious. Squeezing my eyes shut, moving my head away from the menacing hot comb. The gradual sliding down as my mother braids the tender part of my head. It's all worth it! I spray on the African Royale. I love my skin too!

Melanin marries perfectly with the day's Golden Hour. I play sports, my skin has different tones. In the summer, I'm mocha, during the winter, I'm a toffee mocha. A mix. It gets darker when I sit out in the sun. The darker I am, the prettier I feel.

Big soul food feasts. Spicy, flavorful greens—the Red Hot close by. Yams—and I'm not talking about the ones you put marshmallows on in the oven! I mean the rich brown sugar, cinnamon, nutmeg, and that over-the-top hint of vanilla. Creamy macaroni and cheese, fresh out of the oven. Late family evenings in Ohio, when my uncles and aunts sip their spirits, and us kids gnaw on the smoky pork neck bones.

The music, the kind that reaches your soul. A rhythm that takes you back to when everyone was in a band. A song in your heart, a bounce in your step.

My Blackness never suffocating, always my breath of life.

Along the Way

Jen Soriano

I'm racing tumbleweeds down the street, and scanning—always scanning. Speed is my only defense. Is that man looking at me? He is gazing down at the crumbling sidewalk. The road is empty except for the man and the tumbleweeds and one floating plastic bag.

I lock my red Schwinn to a light post. In between two boarded storefronts is my destination: a dojo that was since pushed out of this forlorn strip. I open the door and scan the room: eight women on a blue mat, one man in thick padding in a corner. The smell of sweat assaults me.

The instructors call us into a circle and instead I want to flee. Trembling, I fixate on one woman and her purple-and-red-striped, over-the-knee socks. Sisa is the only other person of color in the room, a stripper who needs to learn workplace self-defense. I'm nineteen and alone and crying, and I have no idea why I'm here.

Sisa looks me in the eye and says, "You're very brave," and I form an attachment to her kindness. With Sisa at my side, I learn to use my voice. I learn to move my arms with force that cuts through pain and fear. I learn to keep scanning, to deescalate, then run away. But I also learn to stop fleeing, to slow down, to affirm my worth and hold my ground.

I had raced across the country, leaving a cold white place for one of softer tones and warmth, though I did not yet know how to stay. That would take a return and a decade to come. But here at this sour-smelling dojo in an as-yet ungentrified Oakland neighborhood, I began. I glimpsed the home that lies in growing safety, among women seeking independence, who needed to wield our weapons along the way.

Driving to Work, I Think, What If I Were a White Man?

Liza Sparks

Would I be a nanny? Would I be a writer? Would I be a survivor of intimate partner abuse? Would I carry Mace? Would my therapist tell me to talk to angels? Would my boyfriend ask how many sexual partners I had before him? Would the man at the shoe store tell me to smile? Would the man at the bar tell me the same roofie joke? Would I shave my legs? Would I wear a bra? Would I use a menstrual cup? Would I pay out of pocket for a pap smear? Would my insurance cover a breast reduction? Would I experience side effects from birth control? Would I wear high heels? Would I paint my fingernails? Would I curl my eyelashes? Would I carry a purse? Would I worry my clothes were too revealing for work? Would I take my shirt off in public? Would I have $49,989.11 in student debt? Would I get bigger tips when I served tables? Would I know about the pink tax? Would I own stocks? Would I have a trust fund? Would I hate myself? Would I have a gym membership? Would I have an eating disorder? Would I have anxiety? Would I have depression? Would anyone ask me *what are you*? Would I have imposter syndrome? Would I cry when I felt like it? Would I be angry? Would I want to be in the military? Would I tell my friends I loved them? Would I hit women? Would I open doors for women? Would I be a feminist? Would I be straight? Would I be polyamorous or monogamous? Would anyone call me a bitch? Would anyone call me a slut? Would anyone tell me to calm down? Would anyone tell me I was making it up?

Only Pinks, Please

ANUPAMA SPENCER

I didn't think about it much until people began to call attention to the color scheme in my clothes. I look at pink frocks in my childhood pictures. My closet was always filled with light-colored clothes. Mostly pinks.

I wore only pinks and pastels, chosen for me, bought for me, thrust upon me. I was told it went with my skin color. I was not encouraged to wear black or any dark colors. Shopping caused me anxiety and dread.

When we went to shop, the yellow silks and blue satins burst in front of my eyes. The black cottons and white linens silently smiled. The local shop knew what I needed. It has been said a thousand times. *Only pinks, please.*

I would admire the embroidery on a green top, the flowers on a blue top, or the lace on a black top. I could only admire, not own, or wear. I would get grunts of disapproval as I reached for anything other than pink.

The shopkeeper pulled the light colors from the stack of colored clothes and laid them out like a deck of cards for us to see. He, in his moment of courage, suggests a mustard-yellow top, ignored. A turquoise one, ignored. A bottle-green one, eruption. *These colors don't suit her brown skin tone—don't you understand?*

Only pinks and pastels go well with brown skin, not black or blue. When you hear a lie a thousand times, it becomes true.

My reality was colored pink. Tainted, twisted, and stained.

Back to the Roots

ELIZABETH SU

When I'm twenty-one, I visit China for the first time. Everyone wants to take their picture with me. A tall, pale, vaguely Chinese-looking woman who can't speak the language and sports sneakers? A photo op too good to pass up. My husband, who is full Chinese, thinks this is hilarious. I'm jealous he can, at the very least, hack his way through a dim sum order with his broken Cantonese. I can't even pronounce my own family name as we ask for directions to the compound where my grandmother grew up. It's famous, the locals tell us; news that never made it across the Pacific. I stare in awe at the hordes of people lining up to look at a picture of my grandmother. No one would guess that the alien standing next to them is her granddaughter.

Split in Half

ELIZABETH SU

It's an odd feeling to gather evidence about your existence. This is what it feels like to be biracial. A constant dissertation about why you are "enough." Self-help gurus keep shoving the mantra "You Are Enough" down my throat, but when you are defending yourself all day, desperately searching for the box that includes both of your races to squeeze into, only to come up empty-handed, you start to wonder if it's really true. To be biracial, by definition, means you are 50 percent one race, 50 percent another. You are split exactly in half. And when you are split in half, how are you ever supposed to feel whole?

Meet the Minority
Victoria Sun

Why is it that when I get good grades, it's because I'm Asian? You act as if a certain nationality requires all other abilities to fade. Since when did an area change the quality of your work? I wasn't aware that a certain area provides you that perk. The region of your parents' birth shouldn't decide what you're worth.

Let me break this down, google the word "chink." Take a look at the top ten results, then tell me what you think. "A small narrow opening, a fissure or crack." Today's society uses this word without checking the facts.

Perhaps it started back in the 1800s when we worked on the railroad. Cheap labor and white superiority were so easily sold. Those who came to live the American dream soon found everything was never as it seems. Fast-forward two centuries. How many Asians in the media remain in your memory?

Performers you love are from all over the world, like a map of the planet being unfurled. Guess who would fill 61 percent? Yet in memory, Asian actors never make a dent. America the beautiful and the brave, centuries later, still depraved. We love the freedom we are allowed to take, but when it comes to others we still don't relate. If your ancestors are not native to the United States, your family at some point had to immigrate.

To an entire culture that was new. So what if we don't know your language too? Does it justify the need to verbalize having our character defamed because we're not exactly the same?

Just because I speak my mind doesn't mean I'm misbehaving. I will not apologize for my Asian *persuasion*. Stop looking at my race to undermine my authority. Because I'll have you know, you're the fucking minority.

136

Cafeteria Tree

Yong Takahashi

On my first day of school, I arrived with rice in a stainless-steel bowl, bulgogi and kimchi. The next day, I had bibimbap. The kids surrounded me, laughing, kicking up dirt into my food, throwing sticks. I didn't know what they were saying but I knew it wasn't good.

They held their noses and they started a squinty eye skit. I grabbed up my small picnic and ran to the other side of the school. I threw the food in the trash can. When my mother asked if I enjoyed lunch, I said yes.

I explained that people here ate sandwiches and pizza. The following week, I had a bologna sandwich and an apple in a paper sack. But the kids weren't nicer to me. I ate in the large, welcoming arms of a tree behind the school.

It still stands today even though the school is shuttered and for sale.

I still stand as well.

Special Education
YONG TAKAHASHI

My parents waited until we moved out of Detroit before they enrolled me in school. I don't remember being registered. My father just drove me to a corner of two roads.

He said, "Remember how to get here. You'll have to find it tomorrow."

The next morning, I was told to go to school. I started crying so my father dropped me off on the same corner we visited the day before.

"The school is down there," he said, pointing to his left. "It's okay to get out."

I followed the other children inside the building. I didn't know where to go. I stood outside the front office until I was pushed inside. I barely spoke English, so I didn't know what they were saying. My little exposure to *The Six Million Dollar Man* and *The Bionic Woman* episodes weren't enough to help me communicate.

They put me in Special Education.

Searching
GRACE TALUSAN

I've always wanted to know what it feels like to blend into the crowd. Growing up, I could count the other families of color in my town on one hand. Initially I sought out the few girls at school who looked like me, adoptees from Korea and China. But we had little in common. After an incident in the first grade, when a third grader danced around me making *ching-chong* sounds while pulling back the corners of his eyes, I did everything I could to be like everyone else. I practiced the Boston accent until it felt like my own. I wore green on St. Patrick's Day to be as Irish as my classmates. I prayed before sleep for God to transform me into a white girl. When I did not wake up blonde and blue-eyed, I changed my prayer: a white girl with brown hair and brown eyes would be okay. Over the years, I've developed a habit of scanning any place I enter—a classroom, a workplace, a party—searching for the faces of people who look like me. I don't expect to find them, but I still look.

Watch Out, There Might Be Spies in the Room

Jeanne Tanaka

Growing up I never felt I was different because I was Japanese. Then when I was seventeen years old Japan bombed Pearl Harbor and my life as I knew it would never be the same. Papa got taken away by the FBI and Mama was crying, telling us that they might come for us next and line us up and shoot us. Trying to calm her down I told her, "Mama, America is not like that. They won't do something like that."

I was right—they didn't shoot us, but they did enact Executive Order 9066 which forced all Japanese to be put into concentration camps. We had around three months while they built the camps to sell or get rid of everything we owned except for what we were able to carry. We still had to go to school, and that is when one of my teachers told the class, "Watch out, there might be spies in the room." There was only one other boy and myself that were Japanese, and everyone turned around and stared at us. That was the moment I felt and knew I was not one of them.

Graduating high school is supposed to be a time to spread your wings, explore the world, explore life. I spent the next four years imprisoned at the Tule Lake Concentration Camp. Camp was horrible, but it was that moment when I was singled out in the classroom for not being white that changed my life.

these hands
Imani Tolliver

the voice box
the brown and red voice box
that came from two brown necks
and two before that
was called a white girl
an oreo

    who you tryin' to be, anyway?

they told me the color of my voice
before i knew the language to fight back
they told me i wasn't one of them
far from who I thought i was

    white girl
    white girl
    you tryin' to be a white girl

but all i knew was my mother's tongue
all i knew came from the alice in wonderland records
that taught me how to read

i tried to abandon
national geographics and dictionaries
pippi and the mysteries and the magazines
for a language that was more acceptable
my mother tongue was a tattoo that i modified
but never abandoned

now, i read aloud
listening to the nuances i've created
the resonance that burnishes the girl voice
with tobacco and time
rum and crying
into this voice you hear now
that sings when no one's looking
to lovers i trust

I took what shame tried to make
into something else,
into someone of my own making
and gave birth
to myself

Auntie's House
Frances Kai-Hwa Wang

He laughed at me and my family for saving and reusing—tofu containers, green onion rubber bands, plastic bags, twist ties, takeout containers, glass jars, cookie tins—and he took it upon himself to secretly throw away all that we had carefully saved and washed and stored away. He thought it made us small and poor to reuse. He was big and rich enough to go out to the store to buy things new.

He opened and ate all the boxes of chocolates people gave us as gifts, "to take them out of circulation," before we could regift them to someone else.

He said he did not have to recycle because he recycled enough in the '70s.

When I speak to Asian American students and tell them that there are people in the world who throw away all the green onion rubber bands and then go out to Office Max to purchase new rubber bands, the entire audience gasps.

At Auntie's house, my world comes full circle. Shoes off at the door. Stacks of tofu containers by the kitchen sink, green onion rubber bands looped on the faucet, plastic bags full of plastic bags, kitchen towels sewn from rice bags. Twist ties in the chopstick drawer, giant soy sauce can under the sink. Auntie greets me wearing a blue monkey Aéropostale sweatshirt I remember my cousin wearing in the '90s. We eat from plastic Hello Kitty bowls and plates, the same ones we used when I was small. The secret cupboard full of candy and red envelopes is still stocked; I checked. When she sees a tear in the knee of my jeans, she tells me to fetch her cookie tin so she can mend it.

"Have you eaten yet?" 你吃飯了嗎? as code.

143

Hapa

Keʻalohi Wang

Our grandma grew up in the green of Kohala. She knew her straight hair and her slanted eyes. She knew her high cheekbones. She didn't hate them, but she loved our golden blond and angelic blue eyes that were a rare sight in rural Kohala. Our mother was a Shirley Temple from Tennessee. When my grandma looked at me, she saw her unspoken dream burst through. My eyes were slanted but light. I was tall enough.

As a young girl, I saw myself whole. Everything belonged in my body. "Hapa" was a learned word. Half. Exotic. I learned that people saw in me the color they wanted, the dream they wanted. And my grandmother, she saw promise when she looked at me. She saw a dream, born through my mom.

Mischling

DURTHY A. WASHINGTON

A post–World War II "occupation baby," I was born in Germany, but made in America.

Specifically, I was born in Nuremberg, site of the infamous Nuremberg Trials, where twenty-three Nazi war criminals were prosecuted for atrocities against Jews and other *Mischlinge*, the Nazi classification for Germans of mixed race.

My parents, too, are criminals for creating a *Mischling* like me.

In Germany, according to the Nuremberg Laws, my mother, a German citizen, is guilty of *Rassenschande* (race defilement) for marrying my father, a Black American soldier, a crime perceived as high treason, punishable by imprisonment or death.

In the United States, according to the Racial Integrity Act of 1924 (which remained in effect until 1967), my parents are guilty of *miscegenation*, a felony punishable "by not less than one nor more than five years" of imprisonment.

Acutely aware that I was "born a crime," I spent my formative years fighting a crippling inferiority complex rooted in guilt, shame, and fear. I realized that, regardless of how I saw myself, society had branded me a misfit, a mongrel, an alien "Other." Gradually, I started to internalize the "tragic mulatto" stereotype perpetuated by films like *Imitation of Life*.

Then I learned a new name to call myself, coined by poet/warrior Audre Lorde: Afro-German. A name that connotes not "either/or," but "both/and"—not divided, but doubled. As I began to identify with other Afro-Germans—Boris Kodjoe, May Opitz, Hans Massaquoi—my identity crisis started to subside.

"The beginning of wisdom is the definition of terms," declared Socrates.

"Blended Makes Us Better," proclaims an ad for "ethnic" hair-care products.

145

And at last, I understand: my challenge was never about choosing sides, but about belonging to myself and being at home in my own skin.

Instilled Confidence
Zinaria Williams

Most of my patients have never had a Black woman surgeon before. I catch the flash of shock in their eyes when I enter the room and introduce myself as the attending physician, while the male resident working under me steps aside. I excuse that initial glint of surprise. I would be amazed to see a Black woman subspecialist, too. But sometimes I catch another readable emotion—judgment that comes in the form of tightened lips and a gaze to the floor.

My parents groomed me to be confident in situations like this. Daddy, a university professor and sculptor, taught me to be a creative thinker. Mommy, a dignified Mississippian and university administrator, stressed poise and decorum. Even her mother, our "Mother Dear," a proud schoolteacher, would assess my diction. "Enunciate your words," she would say.

Nightly affirmations claiming "I am a winner" empowered me to believe that I could do anything, that nothing was too hard for me, that I was inferior to no one. My parents grew up Black and poor. They knew the world would tell me the opposite.

I completed eleven years of medical school and training where I was usually the only Black person in the room. My biggest fear wasn't failure; it was being seen as mediocre. I pushed myself to prove to others that I belonged just as much as they did.

When I encounter a patient who refuses to acknowledge me and my recommendations, it hurts a little. I get through it by summoning my instilled confidence, focusing on the people who brighten with my presence, and remembering that the more patients I see, the fewer there will be who've never had a Black woman surgeon before.

Give Us Our Crowns
Jane Wong

In China, women are inserting tiny plugs into their noses to appear more white. There are also products named "Nose Up Bridge Straightening Beauty Clips" that you can clamp onto your nose for fifteen minutes a day. Just fifteen minutes. The time it takes to severely overcook an over-easy egg. Reports and articles on beauty trends in China say the same thing: China values Western beauty standards. The eyelid surgery, the breast implants, the hair bleaching. What they mean by Western: white. How is this different from US beauty standards?

Something I do not want to admit: all throughout high school, I used a whitening product. It was labeled "brightening." I was convinced the chemicals burned the shit out of my teenage acne. But really, it was a whitening product with niacinamide. It was depleting my pigment. I was disappearing, a translucent jellyfish. Looking at my senior class photo, my pale face floats away from itself, the thinnest sliver of Dove soap down the drain.

The whitening face wash was expensive and Japanese and we'd buy it under the table from a friend of a friend in New York City's Chinatown or at this hole-in-the-wall Asian beauty store in a strip mall in Marlboro, New Jersey. At the beauty store, the women behind the counter peered at me like I was a seahorse in an aquarium—impossible. Questions floated outward in Chinese, like relentless waves, as my mother pulled me forward, closer to the translucent women.

They pried at me like a pickle jar: where did you get your surgery. No surgery. How are your eyes so big. Are you sure they're natural. Have you modeled your eyes before. You'd be a star in China. What is that beauty mark near your neck. Can we fix that. We can fix that.

MAD

Jane Wong

Jane, deceived by _____ time and again, should not _____ but she_____ and slept with curled fists.

The rat catching a ride on the turtle wins _____. Ugly and coarse, but _____.

Beware of strangers who _____ and win your _____ and lick the sweat off your nose in false _____, just to taste their own _____.

Do not trust in owls, in heads that spin. Heads should not spin nor stink, like ammonia in the armpits, like a habit of _____.

Do not pause to watch insects _____ like dangling lights. Their soft speckled bodies, a minutia of buzzing dandelion seeds, have already _____ you in the neck. Blood on their spindle tongues. This is a metaphor for _____.

There are no wolves in this tale. Only handsome _____ with pea-green eyes who will tell you: "You are as soft as _____." Then, they will carefully cut _____ and _____.

Seek only the smallest kindness, of shaking out a pebble from a neighbor's shoe, to do unto others what you _____. Did you swallow _____?

Jane, called "intense." Surely, heads spun, owl-struck, stating: "If only she _____." Called "feisty," "talks too _____ or talks too_____." Often: "Too smart for _____ good," "I never thought you'd be _____, looking like _____," "you have big eyes for a _____," "curiously strong" or "_____weak," or "it's just _____ and it's for the best."

Her hair, though, is the best, and is remarkably like kindling and okay for _____ to touch, light, and ingest in flame, strand by _____. Ignore when she says _____ or _____. This is _____ of Jane.

Jane rubbed salt all over her body to become a dissolving _____ and thusly, rightfully so, _____ right out of this _____ world.

NOTE FROM THE COVER ARTIST
BY JING JING TSONG

I imagined the vast landscape of experiences of the women contributing to this anthology. How do I honor their experiences?

> *i made it up*
> *here on this bridge between*
> *starshine and clay*

The ethereal meeting the tangible—what happens at this intersection? I kept asking, "What being is strong enough to bring the magic of the heavens, together with the weight of the earth? What being is so audacious, they know they can span these worlds?" *They* are the interesting one, *They* are the "bridge," a third body of energy that grows from and blurs the lines of any single definition. A separation between "starshine and clay" doesn't exist. This juncture changes with light and weather, perspective and landscape.

A figure of strong shapes defined by light, moving through space, began to emerge. This figure was more a force of energy than a body with physical restraints. Her powerful light embodies tangible and ethereal spaces. She is grounded to the earth, yet she soars, arms outstretched, claiming her space. She bridges the boundaries that try to define her. Her being is an ever-shifting meeting of heaven and earth.

—

JING JING TSONG is a *New York Times* bestselling picture book illustrator who has illustrated over twenty books. Her digital collages of elements made with traditional block printing and hand drawing celebrate the diverse colors, textures, and experiences of a multicultural world. Jing Jing's work has been on Best Picture Books of the Year lists by the New York Public Library and Bank Street College of Education. Her artwork appears on three United States Postal Service Forever Stamps and has been commissioned by the National Cherry Blossom Festival.

ABOUT THE POET
LUCILLE CLIFTON

*"I learn from living... my text is the world that I live in.
I keep noticing, though. I keep noticing."*[1]

Born in 1936 in DePew, New York, Lucille Clifton was raised in
Buffalo and grew up watching her mother write poetry. A keen
observer, Clifton often wrote about the bond between mother and
daughter—Clifton had six children of her own. Womanhood is a
recurring theme in Clifton's poetry, as is the physicality of the female
body. Her memoir, *Generations*, traces her family lineage back to
Africa and includes her ancestor, Lucy, the first black woman to be
hanged for manslaughter in Virginia.

Clifton attended Howard University before transferring to
SUNY Fredonia in 1955. At Howard, Sterling Brown and Owen
Dodson were among her teachers; Amiri Baraka and James Baldwin
were her classmates. In 1958 Clifton married Fred James Clifton
whom she met through friend and fellow poet, Ishmael Reed.

Clifton published her first book of poetry, *Good Times*, in 1969.
Her poetry rose to prominence when Langston Hughes published her
work in his anthology, *The Poetry of the Negro* (1970). From 1974 to
1985, Clifton served as Maryland's poet laureate, and several of her
poetry collections were selected for a Pulitzer Prize.

Clifton also wrote numerous children's books which celebrated
African American history as well as explored contemporary social
issues. *Everett Anderson's Goodbye* (1984) won the Coretta Scott
King Award.

Whenever Clifton read her poem, "won't you celebrate with
me," poet Toi Derricotte noted "the audience often stood up and, not

---

[1] Alexs Pate, "A Conversation with Lucille Clifton," *Black Renaissance*, vol. 8,
no. 2/3, Institute of African American Affairs, 2008, 12–191.

only applauded, but cheered . . . people of all ages, genders, colors, classes, of all educational levels—from the halls of the academy to the people on the street—related to and understood her anthem." [2]

Clifton died in Baltimore in 2010. Her poetry continues to speak to the hearts of readers everywhere.

Select Titles

Voices, Rochester, NY: BOA Editions, 2008.

Mercy, Rochester, NY: BOA Editions, 2004.

One of the Problems of Everett Anderson, New York: Henry Holt, 2001.

Blessing the Boats: New and Collected Poems 1988–2000, Rochester, NY: BOA Editions, 2000.

The Terrible Stories, Brockport, NY: BOA Editions, 1996.

The Book of Light, Port Townsend, WA: Copper Canyon Press, 1993.

Quilting: Poems 1987–1990, Brockport, NY: BOA Editions, 1991.

Ten Oxherding Pictures, Santa Cruz, CA: Moving Parts Press, 1988.

Next: New Poems, Brockport, NY: BOA Editions, Ltd., 1987.

Good Woman: Poems and a Memoir: 1969–1980, Brockport, NY: BOA Editions, 1987.

Everett Anderson's Goodbye, New York: Henry Holt, 1984.

Sonora the Beautiful, New York: E. P. Dutton, 1981.

Two-Headed Woman, Amherst: University of Massachusetts Press, 1980.

Generations: A Memoir, New York: Random House, 1976.

An Ordinary Woman, New York: Random House, 1974.

Good News About the Earth, New York: Random House, 1972.

Some of the Days of Everett Anderson, New York: Henry Holt, 1970.

Good Times, New York: Random House, 1969.

---

[2] Toi Derricotte, "In Memoriam: Lucille Clifton 1936–2010," *Callaloo*, vol. 33, no. 2, Johns Hopkins University Press, 2010, 374–79.

CONTRIBUTOR NOTES

LORALEE ABERCROMBIE | *Name*

SOCIAL
    Twitter: @ladyabercrombie

When LORALEE ABERCROMBIE isn't writing, she's teaching English to high school students, reading with her son, singing in a band, baking sweet treats, or talking to her carnivorous plants. She writes picture, middle grade, and young adult books.

KARINA L. AGBISIT | *Driving Soundtrack*

"Living in a big city, it can be difficult to connect with other Latinx people and engage with this community. Spanish-language music is an important way for me to stay connected to my family lineage and the Latinx community. No matter where I go, I know I have this music to provide me with a sense of home."

SOCIAL
    Instagram: @passion4planet
    Linkedin: @karina-agbisit

KARINA L. AGBISIT is a writer and developmental editor from Portland, Oregon. Her writing has been published by *Oregon Humanities*, *Ruminate Magazine*, and *Haunted Waters Press*. She holds an MFA in Creative Writing from Portland State University and is completing an MA in Book Publishing.

MARÍA ALEJANDRA BARRIOS | *The First Warm Day of the Year*

SOCIAL
>mariaalejandrabarrios.com
>Twitter: @mariaalebave

MARÍA ALEJANDRA BARRIOS is a Pushcart-nominated writer born in Barranquilla, Colombia. She has a master's degree in creative writing from The University of Manchester. Her stories have been published in places such as *Hobart Pulp*, *Reservoir Journal*, *Cosmonauts Avenue*, *Jellyfish Review*, *Lost Balloon*, *Shenandoah Literary*, *Vol. 1 Brooklyn*, *El Malpensante*, *Fractured Lit*, and *SmokeLong Quarterly*. She was the 2020 SmokeLong Flash Fiction Fellow, and her work has been supported by organizations such as Vermont Studio Center, Caldera Arts Center, and the New Orleans Writing Residency. She's currently at work revising her debut novel.

HALA ALYAN | *This Is Not a Rehearsal*

SELECT TITLES
>*The Arsonists' City*, Boston: Mariner Books, 2021.
>*The Twenty-Ninth Year*, Boston: Mariner Books, 2019.
>*Salt Houses*, Boston: Mariner Books, 2017.
>*Hijra*, Carbondale: Southern Illinois University Press, 2016.
>*Four Cities*, New York: Black Lawrence Press, 2015.

SOCIAL
>Instagram: @hala.n.alyan

HALA ALYAN is a Palestinian American writer and clinical psychologist whose work has appeared in the *New York Times*, *Poetry*, *Guernica*, and elsewhere. Her poetry collections have won the Arab American

Book Award and the Crab Orchard Series. Her debut novel, *Salt Houses*, was published by Houghton Mifflin Harcourt in 2017, and was the winner of the Arab American Book Award and the Dayton Literary Peace Prize. Her second novel, *The Arsonists' City*, was recently published by Houghton Mifflin Harcourt. Hala lives in Brooklyn with her husband and dog.

ANASTACIA-RENEÉ | *exceptional – weightless*

"I wrote these pieces out of the frustration and daily systemic challenges of balancing life as well as micro and macroaggressions hurled at me. The 'weight' of that burden oftentimes feels so heavy and I lighten that load by writing about it for my own voice and to affirm the sometimes-silenced voices others."

SELECT TITLES
    (v.), Boston: Black Ocean Press, 2017.
    Forget It, Black Radish Press, 2017.
    Answer(Me): Argus Press, 2017.

SOCIAL
    anastacia-renee.com
    Instagram: @anastaciarenee5

ANASTACIA-RENEÉ (She/They) is a queer writer, educator, interdisciplinary artist, speaker and podcaster. She is the author of *(v.)* (Black Ocean) and *Forget It* (Black Radish) and, *Here in the (Middle) of Nowhere* and *Sidenotes from the Archivist* forthcoming from Amistad (an imprint of HarperCollins). They were selected by NBC News as part of the list of "Queer Artist of Color Dominate 2021's Must See LGBTQ Art Shows." Anastacia-Reneé was former Seattle Civic Poet (2017-2019), Hugo House Poet-in-Residence (2015-2017), Arc

Artist Fellow (2020) and Jack Straw Curator (2020). Reneé's poetry, fiction and non-fiction have been published and anthologized widely.

JULIE HAKIM AZZAM | *How to Erase an Arab*

"This piece was written for a special issue of Brevity on race and racialization. At the time, I had been struggling to write an academic essay on Palestinian archives and historical erasure and had New York Times articles on the Lebanese civil war on my desk. The headlines became an organizing rubric for me to compose a different kind of piece about how the personal was political."

SELECT TITLES

"Mommy, Do I Have White Skin? Race and Skin Color in Picture Books," *Horn Book Magazine*, 14 November 2016.
"How to Erase an Arab," *Brevity: A Journal of Concise Literary Nonfiction*, no. 53, Fall 2016.
"Pittsburgh's 'Conflict Kitchen' Is Latest Battleground over Palestine, Free Speech, and Criticism of Israel," *Mondoweiss*, 11 November 2014.

SOCIAL

julieazzam.com
Twitter: @julieazzam

JULIE HAKIM AZZAM is the assistant director of the MFA Program in the School of Art at Carnegie Mellon University. After completing a PhD focusing on contemporary postcolonial literature, she's shifted her focus to write mostly about immigration, race, and disability in children's literature. She has published in *Brevity*, the *Best of Brevity*, the *Pittsburgh Post-Gazette*, the *Horn Book Magazine*, and the *Times Literary Supplement*.

MAROULA BLADES | *White-Haired Nana*

SELECT TITLES

" 'We Have Our Songs' and 'Get Out Of Your Way,' " *Caribbean Writer Journal,* vol. 35, Spring 2021.

"Lives on Recycled Paper," *Ake Review*, vol. 7, Winter 2020.

"A Berlin Totem Pole," *Harpy Hybrid Review*, no. 2.5, Fall 2020.

"An Ancestor Guards," *Nothing to Look Forward to But the Past*, edited by Gregory McCartney and Susanna Galbraith, TULCA, 2020.

The World in an Eye, Manchester, UK: Chapeltown Books, 2020.

SOCIAL

poetrykitchen.com
Facebook: @poetrykitchen
Twitter: @m_blades
LinkedIn: @maroula-blades

MAROULA BLADES is an Afro-British writer living in Berlin. She was nominated for the Amadeu Antonio Prize 2019 for her educational multimedia project "Fringe." The project was supported by the Swiss Jan Michalski Foundation for Writing and Literature. Works were published in *The Caribbean Writer, Thrice Fiction, The Freshwater Review, Words with Jam, Midnight & Indigo, Abridged, The London Reader, Stories of Music Vol. 2, So It Goes, Newfound Journal, Harpy Hybrid Review*, and by Peepal Tree Press, among others. In 2020, Chapeltown Books (UK) released her flash fiction collection, *The World in an Eye*, available on Amazon and Barnes & Noble.

KIMBERLY BLAESER | *Consignment - Living Brave*

"In writing creative nonfiction, I find the slight form of flash memoir pushes me to focus on scene and details and to keep the commentary to a minimum. The piece requires restraint in a way similar to poetry and, also similar to poetry, builds by gesture and absence. This suits my own desire not to 'overtell' these moments. In both, the unsaid also leaves more room for the reader."

SELECT TITLES

Resister en Dansant: Ikwi-nimi: Dancing Resistance, Curnier, France: Éditions des Lisières, 2020.
Copper Yearning, Duluth, MN: Holy Cow! Press, 2019.
Apprenticed to Justice, Cromer, UK: Salt Publishing, 2007.
Absentee Indians and Other Poems, East Lansing: Michigan State University Press, 2002.

SOCIAL

kblaeser.org
Facebook: @kimberly.blaeser
Instagram: @kmblaeser

KIMBERLY BLAESER, past Wisconsin Poet Laureate and founding director of Indigenous Nations Poets, is the author of five poetry collections, including *Copper Yearning*, *Apprenticed to Justice*, and the bilingual *Résister en dansant / Ikwe-niimi: Dancing Resistance*. An Anishinaabe activist and environmentalist from White Earth Reservation, Blaeser edited *Traces in Blood, Bone, and Stone: Contemporary Ojibwe Poetry*. Her photographs, picto-poems, and ekphrastic pieces have appeared in exhibits such as *Ancient Light* and *Visualizing Sovereignty*. A professor at UW–Milwaukee and MFA faculty for the Institute of American Indian Arts, in 2021 she received a Lifetime Achievement Award from the Native Writers' Circle of the Americas.

'IOLANI BROSIO | *On Being Made Whole*

SOCIAL

Instagram: @hawkquarias

'IOLANI BROSIO (she/her/'oia) is a māmā, kumu, and aloha 'āina. She is rooted in Maui, Hawai'i and is sustained by the resiliency and mana of her lāhui Hawai'i.

VIVIAN MARY CARROLL | *Unearthing Joy*

"The two debilitating art sessions depicted in 'Unearthing Joy' have long haunted me. I have spoken with disgust at the adult's behavior but the child within me had refused to cave in and cry. During eight revisions, the child calmed, acknowledging the truths at last expressed. The reward is freely appreciating my art and the art of others."

VIVIAN MARY CARROLL, a Cherokee Nation citizen, holds an MFA in Creative Writing from the Institute of American Indian Arts. Her poems appear in *Yellow Medicine Review*. She is currently working on a manuscript.

SAMANTHA CHAGOLLAN | *Mother Tongue*

"This is about my grandmother, Aurora Zazueta Chagollan, matriarch and proud Mexicana whose many talents weren't often lauded but deserved admiration. When I was young, I was puzzled by her refusal to speak English, because it meant she couldn't communicate with any of her grandchildren. We are all half-white, and none of us spoke Spanish. I now have a better appreciation of her insistence, and her pride."

163

SOCIAL
>therestlessraconteur.com
>Instagram: @samchagollan
>LinkedIn: @samchagollan

SAMANTHA CHAGOLLAN is a writer, editor, and storyteller who geeks out on clever copy. As the author of a variety of children's fiction and nonfiction books, she is living out her nerdy childhood dream of getting paid to tell stories for a living. She earned a bachelor's degree in English from Humboldt State University, where she focused her studies on multicultural literature and the Spanish language. Samantha lives in Southern California with her husband, Matt, and two dogs, Chloe and Charlie, who are all extremely good listeners to the tall tales she spins.

VICTORIA CHO | *Alien - Audition*

"The fetishization of East Asian women is connected to the stereotype that we are subservient and passive. We are desired because we are seen as unequal, as bodies that can be dominated. And in our attempts to escape this position, we are willing to endure knives to our faces. The popularity of surgery shows a kind of desperation and a history of suffering."

SOCIAL
>victoriacho.com
>Facebook: @victoriacho
>Instagram: @victoriacho
>Twitter: @msvictoriacho

VICTORIA CHO is a Korean American writer who was born in Virginia. Her writing has appeared in *SmokeLong Quarterly*, *The*

164

Collagist, Apogee Journal, Quarter After Eight, Word Riot, and *Mosaic*. She is a Kundiman Fellow, a VONA/Voices alumna, and was co–fiction editor of *Apogee Journal*. Victoria has received support from Vermont Studio Center and led creative writing workshops for New York Writers Coalition. She lives in New York City.

FELA CORTÉS | *The Color of My Skin*

SOCIAL
> felacortes.com
> Instagram: @hola_fela
> Twitter: @felacortes
> LinkedIn: @felacortes

At the age of five, FELA CORTÉS declared that she wanted to be an author. Today, Fela is an executive producer based in NYC. After listening to Fela create stories for their son, her husband, Fernando, inspired her to write again. This year, Fela was honored to be a remote writing coach at The Telling Room in Portland, Maine.

CARLA CRUJIDO | *Sugar Coated (1979)*

"A child of a mixed marriage, in 1970s America, I was almost always the only brown girl in the various schools I attended. However, it wasn't until I arrived in San Clemente, California, that the color of my skin was brought to my attention as an undesirable attribute. It was also there that I understood for the first time that I was different and that difference was unacceptable."

SELECT TITLES
> "3 Haiku: Executive Order 9066, Intersection, Massacre,"
> *Tinfish 22: Inarticulate Futures*, February 2022.
> "Ocean Boy," *Ricepaper Magazine*, 23 July 2021.
> "Sugar Coated," *Yellow Medicine Review*, Spring 2021.
> "The Suitcase," *The Ana*, vol. 2, Spring 2020.

SOCIAL
> Instagram: @carlacrujido
> Twitter: @carlacrujido

CARLA CRUJIDO is a hapa writer of Filipino, Mexican, Norwegian, and German descent. Her work has appeared in *Yellow Medicine Review, Ricepaper Magazine, Tinfish, The Ana*, and elsewhere. Carla is a graduate of the MFA program at the Institute of American Indian Arts. Originally from San Francisco, she now calls Portland home.

MARGARITA CRUZ | *Are You Sure That Isn't Your Drinking Name?*

SOCIAL
> shortendings.com
> Instagram: @blue_margaritas
> Twitter: @blue_margaritas

MARGARITA CRUZ received her MFA in Creative Writing from Northern Arizona University. She is currently a columnist for *Flagstaff Live!*, serves as vice president of the Northern Arizona Book Festival, and is an assistant editor for Tolsun Books. When she's not reading, writing, or building community, she is often out hiking in the high desert, where she has found a home. Her works can be found or are forthcoming in [PANK], DIAGRAM, and *Rattle*. In 2021, she published her first chapbook, *Amerixana*, with Ignite Press out of Chatham University's MFA program.

ELLA DECASTRO BARON | *A Dagli for the Friend Who Emailed 10K Words—in Ascending [Dis]order—a One-Way Yelling Match of Why Trump Is God's Savior for 'We the Sheeple' and Why I *Must* Agree*

"I trust my tears as wisdom from my body and ancestors. Since the 2016 US presidential election and global pandemic, I'm now learning to trust my anger as a similar rupture and gift. When this person, a 'sister in Christ,' emailed me her hella long rebuke, I did not want to let it go in the name of 'peace.' I rumbled this 'piece' instead: (micro) climate change, a necessary storm."

SELECT TITLES

(Her)oics: Women's Lived Experiences during the Coronavirus Epidemic, edited by Amy Roost and Joanell Serra, Raleigh, NC: Pact Press, 2021.
Itchy Brown Girl Seeks Employment, San Diego, CA: City Works Press, 2009.

SOCIAL

elladecastrobaron.com
Facebook: @ella.d.baron
Instagram: @elladbaron

ELLA DECASTRO BARON is a second-generation Filipina American raised in Coastal Miwok territory (Vallejo, California). Her memoir is *Itchy, Brown Girl Seeks Employment*. She is published in *(Her) oics: Women's Lived Experiences During the Coronavirus Epidemic*, *Anomaly*, *The Rumpus*, and more. Ella teaches at San Diego City College and Brandman University. She also leads workshops, salas, and *kapwa* (deep interconnection) gatherings that aim to reconcile people and the planet through writing, art, joy, movement, food (yes!), and community. She lives and loves on Kumeyaay territory (San Diego, California) with her husband and interracial family. Her favorite preferred pronoun is We.

CAMILLE DUNGY | *A Good Hike*

SELECT TITLES

Guidebook to Relative Strangers, New York: W. W. Norton, 2017.
Trophic Cascade, Middletown, CT: Wesleyan University Press, 2017.
Smith Blue, Carbondale: Southern Illinois University Press, 2011.
Suck on the Marrow, Pasadena, CA: Red Hen Press, 2010.
What to Eat, What to Drink, What to Leave for Poison, Pasadena, CA: Red Hen Press, 2006.

SOCIAL

camilledungy.com
Instagram: @camilledungy
LinkedIn: @camille-dungy

CAMILLE DUNGY is a widely renowned poet, editor, and author. Her collection of personal essays, *Guidebook to Relative Strangers*, was a finalist for the National Book Critics Circle Award. She has also authored four poetry collections, which have received numerous accolades. Her work has appeared in *Best American Poetry*, nearly thirty anthologies, and dozens of print and online venues. She has also been honored with two NAACP Image Award nominations, two Hurston/Wright Legacy Award nominations, and several poetry and prose fellowships. Dungy is currently an English professor at Colorado State. She lives there with her husband and child.

TINA EHSANIPOUR | *More than a Ghost - Pomegranates*

"'More than a Ghost' was inspired by my frustration with not having a Middle Eastern category on the US Census and therefore feeling invisible as Iranian diaspora. 'Pomegranates' was inspired by one of my fondest childhood memories with my grandmother. Pomegranates are not only beloved in my culture, but they also represent how my family taught me to be present in this world—as unapologetically myself."

SELECT TITLES

"Norooz: Springing into the New Year," *South Writ Large Journal*, Spring 2021.

"Next Stop: Dreams," *In Short–The Podcast*, season 1, episode 7, Blanket Fort Productions, 29 April 2021.

"The first time I make ghormeh sabzi," *Nowruz Journal*, vol. 001, 2021.

"Morning," *Five Minute Lit*, July 2021.

"The Revolution Never Ended," *Golden Thread Productions*, August 1999.

SOCIAL

tinaehsanipour.com
Instagram: @tinaehsanipour
Twitter: @tinaehsanipour

TINA EHSANIPOUR is an Iranian-born, California-raised writer and high school English teacher. Her work has appeared in various places, including *Nowruz Journal*, *South Writ Large Magazine*, *In Short–The Podcast*, and *Five Minute Lit*, as well as onstage with Golden Thread Productions. Never outgrowing her childhood obsession with the magical, she enjoys writing fiction with a touch of magic. Tina lives with her husband and twins in the Bay Area, where she can be found experimenting in the kitchen or tweeting about books, teaching, and other random things.

DARA YEN ELERATH | *Epistle from a Poppy to a Cactus – How to Mount a Butterfly - Steam Iron*

DARA YEN ELERATH's debut collection, *Dark Braid* (BkMk Press), won the John Ciardi Prize for Poetry. A Pushcart Prize nominee, her work has appeared in journals such as *The American Poetry Review*, *AGNI*, *Boulevard*, *Plume*, *Poet Lore*, *Hunger Mountain*, and *The Los Angeles Review*, among others. She received her MFA in Poetry from the Institute of American Indian Arts and resides in Albuquerque, New Mexico.

SAFIA ELHILLO | *Self-Portrait with No Flag*

SELECT TITLES
> *Home Is Not a Country*, New York: Make Me a World, 2021.
> Elhillo, Safia and Asghar, Fatimah, editors, *The BreakBeat Poets, Vol. 3: Halal If You Hear Me*, Chicago: Haymarket Books, 2019.
> *The January Children*, Lincoln: University of Nebraska Press, 2017.
> *The Life and Times of Susie Knuckles*: Well&Often, 2012.

SOCIAL
> safia-mafia.com
> Instagram: @safiamafia
> Twitter: @mafiasafia

SAFIA ELHILLO is the author of the novel-in-verse *Home Is Not a Country* and the poetry collection *The January Children*, which received the 2016 Sillerman First Book Prize for African Poets and a 2018 Arab American Book Award. Sudanese by way of Washington, DC, she holds an MFA from The New School, a Cave Canem Fellowship, and a 2018 Ruth Lilly and Dorothy Sargent Rosenberg

Fellowship from the Poetry Foundation. Safia is a Pushcart Prize nominee and was listed in Forbes Africa's 2018 "30 Under 30." She is a 2019–2021 Stegner Fellow at Stanford University.

THERESA FALK | *In Answer to Your Questions as You Pass Our Family on the Street - To My Daughter Reading Tolkien*

"As a Filipinx mother of a white son and Filipino daughter, I am sharply aware of the privileges and burdens they each hold. I wrote these pieces as a celebration of their strength and potential, both as individuals and members of a passionate, loving, and diverse family. My children, Brand and Rebecca, are brilliant stars who will light our future's way. May they do so with love."

SELECT TITLES

"Bear," *Messages of Peace: Words of Inspiration for Everyday Living from Hawaii,* edited by Worth Grace and Lori Chaffin: Inspired Wellness Publishing, 2013.
"Shells," *Hawaii Women's Journal,* Spring 2010.
"Sustenance," *Strong Currents 2,* edited by Kathryn Godwin and Lynn Rae Harris: Aloha Romance Writers, 2006.
"Gardening," *Strong Currents 2,* edited by Kathryn Godwin and Lynn Rae Harris: Aloha Romance Writers, 2006.

SOCIAL

Facebook: @starbreeze
Instagram: @starbreeze9
Twitter: @MrsFalksroom

THERESA FALK (she/her) is a Filipinx educator, writer, and activist. She has taught literature, public speaking, and women's studies at the middle and high school level for almost thirty years. Her poetry and prose have appeared in various publications, and she is a former columnist for *The Hawaii Women's Journal*. Theresa is a mother to two children, Rebecca Lourdes, nine, and Brand Duncan, eight.

ALISON FEUERWERKER | *Eggs*

"I wrote this piece as an exercise in a memoir-writing class, where we were asked to describe a familiar object in a new way. I had also recently participated in a Storytelling for Social Justice workshop. I tried to express the experience of being white-passing and therefore separated from my true self, and how it felt to be seen and known."

SOCIAL
       Instagram: @afeuerwerker

ALISON FEUERWERKER (she/her) is a community musician, activist, and traveler: a mix of Chinese heritage from her mother, Eastern European Jewish heritage from her father, a left-liberal and eccentric American childhood, early adult years living in an intentional community, and a recent year of living and working in Tanzania. She has lived most of the past four decades in Ontario, Canada. Alison is working on a collection of memoirs about growing up in a mixed-race family in the 1960s and '70s.

FATIMAH FINNEY | *In My Skin: An Autobiography*

"This piece has been in my mind, in fragmented parts, for years. The deadline for submissions gave me the opportunity and the urgency to bring it all together. In the midst of a personal journey toward vulnerability and transparency, I was thinking more deeply about my racial identity and its evolution. My submission is an exercise in courage; a step toward being known, on purpose, just a little more."

SOCIAL

>healingdifferently.com
>Instagram: @fatimahfinneylmhc
>LinkedIn: @fatimahfinney

FATIMAH FINNEY is a serial goal-setter, lover of new ideas, and imaginative thinker. She works as a mental health counselor and maintains a private practice serving BIPOC and young adults. As a facilitator and consultant, Fatimah coaches individuals and organizations striving to establish sustainable diversity, equity, and inclusion practices. Fatimah has enjoyed writing since she wrote her first poem in middle school. She has recently tapped back into this creative outlet and is looking forward to sharing more of her personal reflections in the digital space.

CMARIE FUHRMAN | *Cindian – Cindyjawea - Dress Up Like an Indian*

"I wrote this piece in hopes that non-Native people might understand what it is to be Native and female and that the role models that society gives young Native women can confuse and erase their unique cultural and ethnic identity."

SELECT TITLES

>"Camped Beneath the Dam: Poems," *Floodgate Poetry Series*, vol. 6, edited by Andrew McFadyen-Ketchum, Indianapolis, IN: Etchings Press, 2020.
>Fuhrman, CMarie, and Dean Rader, editors, *Native Voices: Indigenous Poetry, Conversation, and Craft*, North Adams, MA: Tupelo Press, 2019.

SOCIAL
> cmariefuhrman.com

CMARIE FUHRMAN is the author of *Camped Beneath the Dam: Poems* (Floodgate, 2020) and co-editor of *Native Voices* (Tupelo, 2019). She has published poetry and nonfiction in multiple journals, including *Emergence Magazine, Yellow Medicine Review, Cutthroat: A Journal of the Arts, Whitefish Review, Broadsided Press, Taos International Journal of Poetry and Art*, as well as several anthologies. CMarie is a regular columnist for the *Inlander*, the translations editor for *Broadsided Press*, nonfiction editor for *High Desert Journal*, and director of the Elk River Writers Conference. She resides in the mountains of West Central Idaho.

HELENA GARCIA | *A Tale I Have Never Lived*

"That memory was so well hidden in my mind that I only perceived it last year. Writing it down was an acknowledgment of my identity and the barriers and bias I went through and overcame. I aim to become a representative for those who are overlooked by society, to create change so they can have a space to be seen and heard."

SELECT TITLES
> *Meninas que Escrevem*, edited by Nós Marias Coletivo, *Jandaíra*, 2020.
> *Nature*, 2020-2021

SOCIAL
> Instagram: @lehgarciafhs
> Twitter: @lehgarciafhs
> LinkedIn: @ahelenagarcia

HELENA GARCIA is a seventeen-year-old black girl from Pernambuco, Brazil. When she was going through a hard time, writing taught her how to survive, and poetry teaches her how to keep living. She is one of the co-authors of the book, *Meninas Que Escrevem* (Girls Who Write), and publishes her poetry on Instagram. Writing has been Helena's passion for her whole life, especially poetry and nonfiction. She uses it to help, connect with, and impact people. Garcia also loves performing. In her free time, Helena watches TV, hangs out with her friends, and cooks new recipes.

ISABEL GARCIA-GONZALES | *Pull*

"I wrote 'Pull' in the midst of the pandemic after participating in a workshop series for Filipinx folks, Wayfinding in a Time of Transformation, which explored themes of decolonization, authenticity, and internalized oppression. Kayaking for the first time connected me to my seafaring ancestors, and at the same time I began to imagine myself as a future ancestor, whose life in the Filipinx diaspora is worthy and authentic too."

SOCIAL
isabelgarciagonzales.com
Instagram: @beginners_shine

ISABEL GARCIA-GONZALES is a writer, artist, educator, facilitator, and fledgling comics maker. She has received fellowships, residencies, and awards for her writing, including support from Hedgebrook, VONA/Voices, and the Bread Loaf Writers' Conference. Isabel's work has appeared in publications including *Kuwento: Lost Things, An Anthology of New Philippine Myths*, and *riksha: Asian American Creative Arts in Action*. A core organizer of Banyan: Asian American

175

Writers Collective, Isabel lives in the Chicago area with her partner and three children and is at work on a novel and a collection of fledgling comics about her life in the Filipinx/Asian American diaspora.

GABRIELLE GHADERI | *Persian vs. Iranian*

SOCIAL

gabrielleghaderi.com
LinkedIn: @gabrielle-ghaderi

GABRIELLE GHADERI is an Iranian American writer who writes about her experiences growing up between two cultures. She hopes to connect with other multiethnic individuals through her exploration of existing in the in-between.

VICTORIA K. GONZALES | *Part of the Problem*

"My piece is one I didn't expect to write, yet one I was sure I had to, reflecting on 2020—specifically, the blatant racism I've heard my entire life. It was during the presidential election, when family and friends revealed nasty truths about themselves to the world through social media posts. The disregard for their own family, closest friends, and humanity, shocked me, hurt me, angered me, and has revealed to me that there is no room for silence; although I once was, in order to keep the peace between loved ones and myself, I will not be silent anymore."

SELECT TITLES

"Born Again," *Heavy Feather Review*, 2020.
"Sister," *Remembering What We Carry Anthology*, edited by the Institute of American Indian Arts, IAIA Anthology, 2020.

SOCIAL
> Instagram: @victoryia.gonzales09

VICTORIA K. GONZALES has spent most of her days with a book in one hand and pen in the other. She graduated from Santa Fe High, where she found poetry and journalism, then received her BFA and MFA from the Institute of American Indian Arts, where she majored in creative writing with a focus on fiction. When she's not creating surreal short stories, she's running around the land of enchantment with her fiancé, writing scripts, or studying the works of Tarantino, Smith, Anderson, Ritchie, Wright, and Waititi. She has two dogs and two cats. She loves to laugh.

MICHELLE GUERRERO HENRY | *The Cartography of My Face*

"My micro essay was inspired by The Face: Cartography of the Void by Chris Abani. Having spent years wishing I could change my appearance, his meditation on his face had me consider mine, contemplating the reasons behind the shame and pride that twists inside so many of us. I wanted to capture how I learned to love myself when I looked more closely into the past."

SOCIAL
> michelleghenry.com
> Instagram: @michelleghenry

MICHELLE GUERRERO HENRY is a Cuban/Ecuadorian writer living in an old farmhouse just outside NYC. She is a 2016–2018 Think Write Publish Fellow, 2017 VONA Fellow, as well as a Writing Our Lives alum. Her work has appeared in *Longleaf Review*, *Lifting the Burden of Shame Series* with Wendy Angulo Productions, and *Hispanecdotes*.

She is an MFA candidate in Creative Writing at Randolph College and a Nancy Craig Blackburn '71 Fellow.

SAMINA HADI-TABASSUM | *Hair/Bhaal*

SOCIAL

saminahaditabassum.com

SAMINA HADI-TABASSUM is a professor at Erikson Institute in Chicago. Her first book of poems, *Muslim Melancholia* (2017), was published by Red Mountain Press. She has published poems in *East Lit Journal, Journal of Postcolonial Literature, Papercuts, Mosaic, Main Street Rag, Tin House*, and *riksha: Asian American Creative Arts in Action*. She has published short stories in *New Orleans Review, Chicago Quarterly Review*, and *Louisville Review*.

STEPHANIE HAN | *Passing in the Middle Kingdom*

"'Passing in the Middle Kingdom' is the titular piece of my manuscript, a Wilder Prize finalist. As a Korean American in a Hong Kong village, I passed as Chinese. My writing from this time explored my marriage's collapse, the fatigue and joy of motherhood, and the desire for home and belonging."

SELECT TITLES

Swimming in Hong Kong, Spokane, WA: Willow Springs Books, 2017.

SOCIAL

drstephaniehan.com
Facebook: @hawaii.stephaniehan

Instagram: @drstephaniehan
Twitter: @drstephaniehan
LinkedIn: @stephanie-han
YouTube: @TheBuddhafun

STEPHANIE HAN teaches writing workshops at drstephaniehan.com. Her poetry manuscript, *Passing in the Middle Kingdom*, is a Wilder Prize finalist. She authored *Swimming in Hong Kong*, recipient of the Paterson Fiction Prize, finalist for AWP's Grace Paley Prize, the Spokane Prize, and the Asian Books Blog Award. A PEN and VONA fellow, she received grants from the LA Department of Cultural Affairs and was the inaugural English Lit PhD of City University of Hong Kong. She lives in Hawaiʻi, home of her family since 1904.

IDA SOON-OK HART | *Elegy - Kkamdoongie in Korea, Kolored in Kentucky, A Chink in America*

SOCIAL
Facebook: @ida.hart.3
LinkedIn: @Ida-Hart

IDA SOON-OK HART is a Korean War baby that was sent to live with her Black father in the segregated South in 1961. Her education includes a BA from Antioch College in Ohio and an MS in education from Mount Saint Mary's in Los Angeles. She was a *Writer's Digest* competition winner in 2017, 2018, and 2019, with publications in three anthologies for women of color. Now retired as an educator, she is working on her memoir. Her volunteer service is sponsoring and supporting women suffering from alcoholism and addiction.

SADIA HASSAN | *Reader, I Hadn't Named It, Yet*

SOCIAL
> Facebook: @sadia.hassan.5817300
> Instagram: @blckrdaberry
> Twitter: @blckrdaberry

SADIA HASSAN is the author of *Enumeration* (Akashic Books, 2020), part of the *New-Generation African Poets: A Chapbook Set*. Winner of the 2020 Hurston/Wright College Writers Award, Hassan currently writes and teaches in Oxford, Mississippi, where she is pursuing her MFA at the University of Mississippi. More of her work can be found in The American Academy of Poetry, *Boston Review*, *Longreads*, and elsewhere.

LISA LEE HERRICK | *Greetings from the Land of Smiles*

"This micro essay was inspired by a real confrontation in San Francisco. It was my first time dating someone who looked like me. I had assumed that our shared experiences with racism would provide mutual comfort—but I quickly learned the painful difference between assimilation and acculturation, and that Asian Americans are neither a monoculture nor a monolith."

SELECT TITLES
> "Written in the Language of Flowers," *Catapult*, 8 February 2022.
> "The Joy of Being a Bad Asian," *Medium*, 9 July 2021.
> "I Am Not Your Peril," *Emergence Magazine*, 29 April 2020.
> "We Learned to Fear Tiger and to Love Squirrel," *Emergence Magazine*, 11 October 2019.
> "The Abattoir," *The Rumpus*, 29 May 2018.

SOCIAL

lisaleeherrick.com
Facebook: @lisaleeherrick
Twitter: @lisaleeherrick

LISA LEE HERRICK is an award-nominated Hmong American writer, artist, and media producer based in California. She is a PEN America Emerging Voices Fellow, and her memoir in essays was named a finalist for the Restless Books Prize for New Immigrant Writing.

CHELSEA TAYRIEN HICKS | *Beige Mask #1 - Beige Mask #2*

"I grapple with accepting my skin color. My ancestral profile is similar to Jean Toomer's, an author known for the abandonment of his own communities enabled by light skin color. Some of my ancestors made the passing journey from 'mulatto' to 'white' in two generations, while others were born of Osage-French intermarriage. As a woman carrying European, Indigenous, and African ancestors, my body requires me to voice the unsayable."

SELECT TITLES

A Calm & Normal Heart, Los Angeles: Unnamed Press, 2022.
"LA NA or the Wazhahze is Word for Guilt," *The Audacity*, 2021.
"Ritual," *Yellow Medicine Review*, Spring 2021.
"Khadijah Britton Is Still Missing," *Indian Country Today*, 25 March 2020.
"The Living Wound," *The Rumpus*, 11 February 2017.

SOCIAL

Instagram: @chelseatayrien

CHELSEA TAYRIEN HICKS (Osage, Pawhuska District) is a recent graduate from the Institute of American Indian Arts and a 2020 finalist for the Eliza So Fellowship for Native American women writers. She is co-composer of the sound art piece "Onomatopoeias for Wrangell-St. Elias," a 2016 and 2017 Writing By Writers Fellow, and a 2016 Wah-Zha-Zhi Woman Artist of the Osage Nation Museum. Her stories and essays have been published in *McSweeney's*, *Indian Country Today*, *The Rumpus*, *Yellow Medicine Review*, *The Believer*, and elsewhere. She is of Osage, Cherokee, Shawnee, mixed Cajun, French, German, and Scottish descent.

CHRISTINE C. HSU | *China Doll*

"I still have mixed emotions about this moment in my past. I've never told my friend about this interaction I had with her mom, and don't know if I ever will. The play, *China Doll* by Elizabeth Wong, inspired the title of my micro essay."

SOCIAL
medium.com/@hsu.christine
Twitter: @HsuChristineC
LinkedIn: @hsuchristine

CHRISTINE C. HSU is a writer, playwright, and poet based in Oakland, California. She has been published by *The Bold Italic*, *xoJane*, *KQED*, *ABC News Radio Online*, *Yellow Arrow Journal*, *Lunchbox Moments*, *Slipform Poetry Anthology 2020*, and *DropOut Literary Magazine*. Her play, *I Love You But . . .*, was a finalist in the Negro Ensemble Company 10 Minute Play Competition, and her play *Faith* was a finalist for the Crafton Hills College New Works Festival 2021.

KAITLYN HSU | *Lunch*

"I want to tell my younger self to be grateful and embrace those things that made her different from everyone else, like pouring soy sauce over fried eggs, wearing cheap slippers around the house, or having a Chinese middle name people can't pronounce. I want her to know that the food she's eating has a story and is a hundred times more valuable than anything purchased at the store."

SOCIAL
>Facebook: @kaitlyn.hsu.5
>Instagram: @kait.hsu
>LinkedIn: @kaitlyn-hsu

KAITLYN HSU is a business student studying at the University of Arizona in Tucson. A proud third-generation Chinese American, she writes novels and flash fiction in her free time. She is also a visual and digital artist, for which she has won awards.

ROGELIA LILY IBARRA | *Érase una Nariz Superlativa*

"The title (translated), 'It Was a Superlative Nose,' is from the sonnet, 'A un hombre de gran nariz,' ('To a Big-Nosed Man') by Francisco de Quevedo, and was inspired by personal and literary histories. It was liberating to write, as it helped me understand the intersecting narratives that bind and define our bodies and how we experience and navigate cultures, their tensions and violence. The body is a palimpsest of histories to be conjured, remembered, negotiated, reclaimed, and resisted."

SOCIAL
>LinkedIn: @rogelio-lily-ibarra

The daughter of Mexican immigrants and Chicagoan, ROGELIA LILY IBARRA holds a PhD in Spanish Studies and enjoyed teaching about languages and literatures for eighteen years. Ibarra has an eclectic research background that allowed her to code-switch through various disciplines covering areas such as women's literary, political histories, and Mexican/Latinx popular culture. Her recent work explores topics like toxic masculinity, meritocracy, motherhood, ancestral healing, folklore, and mental health awareness.

MEE OK ICARO | *Real Mom*

SELECT TITLES
"A Paradoxical Apocalypse: Werner Herzog's La Soufrière," *Bennington Review*, vol. 9, forthcoming.
"Rear Window," *Prairie Schooner*, forthcoming.
"Queer Seoul," *Witness Magazine*, Fall 2021.
"Parasite to Coronavirus," *LA Times,* 9 April 2020.
"Ayahuasca Let Me Walk Again," *Medium,* 29 May 2018.

SOCIAL
mee-ok.com

MEE OK ICARO is an award-winning literary prose stylist and occasional poet. She is the winner of the inaugural Prufer Poetry Prize, runner-up in the Prairie Schooner Creative Nonfiction Contest, and a finalist for the Scott Merrill Award for poetry as well as the Annie Dillard Award for Creative Nonfiction. Her writing has appeared, or is forthcoming, in the *LA Times, Boston Globe Magazine, Georgia Review, Bennington Review, River Teeth, Witness, Pleiades,* Michael Pollan's "Trips Worth Telling" anthology, and elsewhere. She is also featured in *[Un]Well* on Netflix and working on a forthcoming memoir.

AMAL IMAN | *Hyper/in/visible - R/evolution*

"These pieces are love letters: to me, to Pride, to everyone queer and Muslim. Within them, I seek to capture the complexities and nuances of existing at the intersection of two marginalized identities, which are rendered both invisible and hypervisible. I wrote to speak us into existence, as a celebration of the courage it takes to exist proudly when you're told you shouldn't."

AMAL IMAN is a fierce believer in storytelling as a form of activism, and aims to provoke empathy, understanding, and ultimately inspire change through her words.

TONI JENSEN | *Women in the Fracklands*

SELECT TITLES
   Carry, New York: Ballantine Books, 2020.
   From the Hilltop, Lincoln: Bison Books, 2010.

SOCIAL
   tonijensen.com
   Instagram: @tonijensen3086
   Twitter: @ToniJens

TONI JENSEN is the author of the memoir *Carry* and the short story collection *From the Hilltop*. She teaches at the University of Arkansas and the Institute of American Indian Arts. She is Métis.

ALYSSA JOCSON PORTER | *Collector's Item*

SOCIAL
Twitter: @itsuhLEEsuh

ALYSSA JOCSON PORTER is a Filipina American writer, with a bachelor's degree in creative writing from Seattle University and a master's in library and information science. Her short-form writing has been featured in SixWordMemoirs.com and *The Daily Drunk*, and she is currently drafting a collection of micro essays about her big Filipino family. In addition to writing creative nonfiction, she teaches information literacy as a community college librarian. Alyssa lives in Seattle/Duwamish land with her husband, Joe, and their two Chihuahua mixes, Astro and Ursa.

ANITA JOHNSON | *Combative*

ANITA JOHNSON is a female Black Southern writer and poet who brings characters to life to tell stories not often told of our past and create futures inclusive of many cultures and perspectives. She writes fiction and nonfiction for young adults and adults. As a former English teacher, she aims to write stories that can ignite imaginations and inspire students to read. Anita holds a BA in English from Mount Holyoke College and continues to elevate her writing craft. She founded an online global space for Black creative writers to explore, write, and share. She currently lives in Knoxville, Tennessee.

186

TAYARI JONES | *Black Everything*

SELECT TITLES

> *An American Marriage*, Chapel Hill: Algonquin Books, 2018.
> *Silver Sparrow*, Chapel Hill: Algonquin Books, 2011.
> *The Untelling*, New York: Warner Books, 2005.
> *Leaving Atlanta*, New York: Warner Books, 2002.

SOCIAL

> tayarijones.com
> Facebook: @tayarijones
> Instagram: @tayari
> Twitter: @tayarijones

New York Times best-selling author TAYARI JONES is the author of four novels, most recently *An American Marriage*. A 2021 Guggenheim Fellow, Jones has also been a recipient of the Hurston/Wright Legacy Award, United States Artist Fellowship, NEA Fellowship, and Radcliffe Institute Bunting Fellowship. Her third novel, *Silver Sparrow*, was added to the NEA Big Read Library of classics in 2016. Jones is a graduate of Spelman College, University of Iowa, and Arizona State University. She is an Andrew D. White Professor-at-Large at Cornell University and the Charles Howard Candler Professor of Creative Writing at Emory University.

LEENA JUN | *Dear White Evangelicals*

SOCIAL

> reveleena.com

LEENA JUN is the pseudonym for a Korean American neophyte writer in Southern California who wears many hats. She has worked as an adjunct professor, consultant, and designer but has always carried a torch for writing. She is currently working on her first novel.

KRISTIANA KAHAKAUWILA | *Brown Baby - Stranger Danger*

SELECT TITLES
This is Paradise, London; New York: Hogarth, 2013.

SOCIAL
kristianakahakauwila.com
Facebook: @kristianakahakauwila

KRISTIANA KAHAKAUWILA is a hapa writer of kanaka maoli, German, and Norwegian descent. Her first book, *This is Paradise: Stories* (Hogarth, 2013), takes as its heart the people and landscapes of contemporary Hawai'i. Kristiana is an assistant professor at University of Hawai'i at Mānoa, and also teaches in the low-residency MFA at the Institute of American Indian Arts. She is currently at work on a novel set on the island of Maui.

MOHJA KAHF | *Voyager Dust*

SELECT TITLES
Hagar Poems, Fayetteville: University of Arkansas Press, 2016.
The Girl in the Tangerine Scarf, New York: PublicAffairs, 2006.
E-mails from Scheherazad, Gainesville: University Press of Florida, 2003.
Western Representations of the Muslim Woman: From Termagant to Odalisque, Austin: University of Texas Press, 1999.

SOCIAL
> Twitter: @ProfKahf

MOHJA KAHF has been a professor of comparative literature and Middle Eastern studies at the University of Arkansas since 1995. She is author of the novel *The Girl in the Tangerine Scarf*, two other poetry collections, *Hagar Poems* and *E-mails from Scheherazad*, and a nonfiction work, *Western Representations of the Muslim Woman: From Termagant to Odalisque*. She has won the Pushcart Prize and an Arkansas Arts Council Individual Artist Award. She is a founding member of the Radius of Arab American Writers and has served on the board of the Ozark Poets and Writers Collective in Fayetteville, Arkansas.

BLAISE ALLYSEN KEARSLEY | *The First Time It Happened*

"This was the first time I realized I was 'other,' though I wouldn't learn that term until at least a decade later. It was a moment of strange crystallization; I knew I didn't look the way my mom looked and I didn't look the way my dad looked either, and now there was something inherently problematic about that. It was also the moment that I became unapologetically proud of who my father is."

SOCIAL
> blaiseallysenkearsley.com
> Facebook: @blaiseallysen
> Instagram: @blaiseallysen
> Twitter: @blaiseallysen

BLAISE ALLYSEN KEARSLEY (she/her) is a Black-biracial writer. She teaches creative nonfiction writing, and is the creator, producer, and host of *How I Learned*, a live series featuring new and established writers, storytellers, and comedians. She lives in New York.

LENA KHALAF TUFFAHA | *What Do We Call It?*

SELECT TITLES
> *Letters from the Interior*, Richmond, VA: Diode Editions, 2019.
> *Arab in Newsland*, Kingston, WA: Two Sylvias Press, 2017.
> *Water & Salt*, Pasadena, CA: Red Hen Press, 2017.

SOCIAL
> lenakhalaftuffaha.com
> Twitter: @LKTuffaha

LENA KHALAF TUFFAHA is a poet, essayist, and translator. Her first book, *Water & Salt* (Red Hen Press), won the 2018 Washington State Book Award. Her chapbook, *Arab in Newsland*, won the 2016 Two Sylvias Press Prize. She is the recipient of a 2019 Artist Trust Fellowship and has served as the inaugural Poet-In-Residence at Open Books: A Poem Emporium, in Seattle. She holds a BA in comparative literature from the University of Washington and an MFA from the Rainier Writing Workshop at Pacific Lutheran University.

SABINA KHAN-IBARRA | *Hues of Mama*

"My inspiration for this piece was my mother. Only after I became a mother did I recognize and admire her strength. How she responded to difficult moments shaped me and I try to teach my children, especially my daughter, to understand her strength and worth and to approach the world from that space."

SOCIAL

> shuffle.do/@sabina
> Facebook: @sabinakhanibarrawriter
> Instagram: @sabinakhanibarra_writes
> Twitter: @sabina_writes

SABINA KHAN-IBARRA is a Pashtun American, Muslim writer. A recent San Francisco State University graduate with an MFA in Creative Writing (Distinguished Honors), her poems are published in *iO* Literary magazine, *Show Us Your Papers*, a book about being othered in America, and other publications. A chapter from her upcoming novel, *Poppy Flower*, can be found in an anthology called *Taboos and Transgression* (Madville Publishing, 2021). Sabina is the recipient of the Joe Brainard Creative Writing Fellowship, the Wilner Award in Short Fiction, and first place in the Martha's Vineyard Fellowship. She resides in Northern California with her husband, two children, five hens, and four rabbits.

SAHELI KHASTAGIR | *Whose Skin Is My Skin?*

"Whenever I go home, my mother tends to my body with food, face-packs, drinks, vitamin pills, hair oils, etc. I used to find this irritating when I was younger, but now I see myself the way she does—as the body she made and cared for. I also see my body as loved and claimed by others, who see beauty where she might see a marring of her craft."

SOCIAL

> sahelikhastagir.com
> Instagram: @sahelikhastagir
> LinkedIn: @saheli-khastagir

SAHELI KHASTAGIR is a painter, writer, and development professional from India, based in New Orleans.

AMANDA MEI KIM | *Touch: A Transcription*

"My writing explores how we are bound together by both human-designed systems and our transcendent need for love and connection. In this essay, I draw linkages between urban planning, racism in our food supply chain, xenophobia in our pandemic response, interracial violence, interracial love, and human touch. I explore valuation and the currency of human dignity, which should flow freely, with no limitations for any of us."

SOCIAL
> amandameikim.com
> Instagram: @amandameikim
> Twitter: @amandameikim

AMANDA MEI KIM is a Japanese and Korean American who grew up on a family farm in California. She writes about rural communities of color. She received her BA in American studies from Brown University and her MFA in Creative Writing from San Francisco State University. She received the Phelan Literary Award, was a finalist for the Heekin Award, and was nominated for a Pushcart Prize. Amanda completed residencies at Yefe Nof, Hedgebrook, and the Fine Arts Work Center. Her work has been published in *Tayo*, *Brick*, *LitHub*, and *PANK*.

EUGENIA KIM | *Broad Margins*

"I was emerging from the subway when a man hollered 'Konichiwa' at me, twice. It reminded me of the myriad ways I've been tagged as

Asian, and how I had once capitalized on this during a dark period in my past when I was unaware of the pain of otherness I was self-inflicting. This essay brought it back into my own power."

SOCIAL
> eugenia-kim.com
> Facebook: @EugeniaKimAuthor
> Instagram: @eugeknee
> Twitter: @Eugenia_Kim

EUGENIA KIM's debut novel, *The Calligrapher's Daughter*, won the Borders Original Voices Award, was shortlisted for the Dayton Literary Peace Prize, and was a Washington Post Best Historical Novel and Critic's Pick. Her second novel, *The Kinship of Secrets*, was a Library Reads pick, and an Amazon Best Book of the Month / Literature and Fiction. Both were also published in the UK and elsewhere. She teaches at Fairfield University's MFA Creative Writing Program.

IRIS (YI YOUN) KIM | *jjimjilbang—bathhouse*

"I wrote this after I moved in with my parents during the pandemic. After a few months, I had grown much closer to my mother than ever before. I also started going to therapy to process a sexual assault that had happened to me years earlier. I started to view my mother's body with awe—the strength and the grace it holds—and allowed myself forgiveness for all the violence that had been inflicted upon my own."

SELECT TITLES
> "The Hybrid Korean-English Language of 'Minari' Makes It Feel Like Home," *Electric Literature*, 1 April 2021.
> "The History Behind California's Battle Over Ethnic Studies," *Time*, 15 September 2020.

"A Non-Whitewashed History of the 19th Amendment and Women's Right to Vote," *Zora Magazine*, 17 August 2020.
"A Revelation on Mother's Day," *New York Times Modern Love*, 19 May 2020.
"Killing Affirmative Action Won't Fix Harvard's Prejudiced Admissions," *Slate*, 15 August 2018.

SOCIAL

iris-kim.com
Facebook: @iris.kim97
Instagram: @iris.kim7
Twitter: @iris_kim7
LinkedIn: @iriskim1

IRIS (YI YOUN) KIM is a writer and recent USC graduate based out of the West Coast. Her work has appeared in *NYT Tiny Love Stories*, *Slate*, *Time*, *Business Insider*, and *Zora*. In particular, she likes to write about Asian American identity, politics, and culture. In her free time, Iris likes to listen to podcasts on long runs, review books on Goodreads, and make music with her little brother.

KALEHUA KIM | *The Path - The Quirky Sidekick of Color Asks Her Book Club to Pick a Book - When I Am Homesick*

"I am inspired by the pure nature of storytelling. In an effort to help my stories resonate, I wanted to place readers within the spaces I've navigated. These essays are the result of much reflection as I sat alone in those spaces. They are glimpses in the mirror. They are invitations. I hope you can take a moment to look deeper, too."

SOCIAL
kalehuakim.com
Facebook: @kalekim
Instagram: @kalehuakim
Twitter: @kalekim
LinkedIn: @kalehua-kim

KALEHUA KIM is a poet living in the Seattle area. Born of Hawaiian, Chinese, Filipino, and Portuguese descent, her multicultural background informs much of her work. Her poems have appeared in *Belletrist*, *Panoply*, and *ʻŌiwi, A Native Hawaiian Journal*.

LYDIA KIM | *Or Are You Normal*

"In 2021, I was reeling from the spiking violence against Asian Americans, in Atlanta, small towns, against our elders. It was the latest in a long history of violence. I hated not being able to protect my parents every minute. At the same time, I was aging myself, having turned fifty during the pandemic, and fearing my own growing vulnerability, praying my risk would not intensify but knowing it probably would."

SOCIAL
Twitter: @elliswkim

LYDIA KIM is a writer based in the Bay Area. Her work has appeared in *Catapult*, *HAD*, *Longleaf Review* and in the anthology *And If That Mockingbird Don't Sing*. She's an alum of the 2021 Tin House Summer Workshop in fiction and is working on her first novel.

YI SHUN LAI | *Currents*

"Professional jealousy is one thing. It's quite another to be jealous of someone's leisure activities. I needed to explore what was behind my green-eyed glare at Erik's canoe trip. 'Currents' helped me to get there and to explore what was beneath the surface emotion. What I found out is that what Erik took for granted, I'd had to fight for, all my life."

SELECT TITLES
> *Pin Ups*, Stonington, CT: Little Bound Books, 2020.
> *Not a Self-Help Book: The Misadventures of Marty Wu*, Albany, NY: Shade Mountain Press, 2016.

SOCIAL
> thegooddirt.org
> Instagram: @yishunlai
> Twitter: @gooddirt
> LinkedIn: @thegooddirt

YI SHUN LAI is the author of *Pin Ups*, a micro-memoir about her long, ragged relationship with outdoors sport (Homebound Publications, 2020). She is the features editor at *Undomesticated Magazine* and teaches in the MFA program at Bay Path University. She is a diversity, equity, inclusion, and access educator. Find her on Twitter @ gooddirt.

CASSANDRA LANE | *We Are Bridges*

"This is an excerpt from my memoir, *We Are Bridges*, which weaves my contemporary story of romance and becoming a mother with the racist murder of my great-grandfather Burt Bridges, who was lynched in or around 1904 while the love of his life, Mary Magdalene Magee, was pregnant with their son, my mother's father. In writing about this trauma, I wanted to capture what beautiful and good things were also lost through oppression and erasure."

SOCIAL
> cassandralane.net
> Facebook: @cassandralaneauthor
> Instagram: @cassandra.lane71
> Twitter: @casslanewrites
> LinkedIn: @cassandra-lane-717ab331

CASSANDRA LANE is author of *We Are Bridges: A Memoir* (Feminist Press), winner of the Louise Meriwether First Book Prize, and editor in chief of *L.A. Parent* magazine. Her storytelling has appeared in various publications, including *Writers Resist*, the *New York Times'* "Conception" series, *Entropy*, and *The Millions*.

DEVI S. LASKAR | *Girl as Map - I Words*

"I wrote 'Girl as Map' as part of a micropoetry series sponsored by Kaya Press and 18millionrising.org to combat the Muslim Ban in the Trump administration. I wrote 'I Words' to remember the eleventh anniversary of the time when my spouse was racially targeted by his former employer in Georgia and how it has severely impacted my family since 2010."

SELECT TITLES
> *Circa*, Boston: Houghton Mifflin Harcourt Press, 2022.
> *The Atlas of Reds and Blues*, Berkeley, CA: Counterpoint Press, 2019.
> *Anastasia Maps*, Georgetown, KY: Finishing Line Press, 2017.
> *Gas & Food, No Lodging*, Georgetown, KY: Finishing Line Press, 2017.

SOCIAL
   devislaskar.com
   Twitter: @devislaskar
   Instagram: @devislaskar
   LinkedIn: @devi-s-laskar

DEVI S. LASKAR is a poet, photographer, novelist, and former newspaper reporter. Her debut novel, *The Atlas of Reds and Blues*, won the Asian/Pacific American Award for Literature and the Crook's Corner Book Prize. The *Washington Post* named her novel one of the 50 Best Books of 2019. A native of Chapel Hill, North Carolina, Laskar now lives in California with her family.

SHERILYN LEE | *BUR to SJC: On Being an Only Child and Caregiving Road Warrior at 52 - Gray Matter*

"An only child, I chose not to have children for a life of freedom and self-sufficiency. Then one after another, my family got sick and needed care. My father is my fourth care recipient in less than five years. I write about caregiving to give voice to its demands, heartbreak, and isolation. I hope my experience allows other caregivers to feel heard and encourages families to plan for this possibility."

SELECT TITLES
   "The Things I've Done to Avoid Writing This Page," *Brevity*,
   29 March 2019.
   "Summer Solstice," *Angels Flight • literary west*, 20 June 2016.
   "The Personal Assistant Speaks," *Angels Flight • literary west*,
   17 June 2016.

SOCIAL
>sherilynlee.com
>Facebook: @sherilynwrites
>Instagram: @sherilywrites
>Twitter: @sherilynwrites

SHERILYN LEE earned her Master of Fine Arts in Creative Nonfiction from Antioch University Los Angeles. She posts daily #overheards to her popular Instagram channel, where she also writes about being a family caregiver. Sherilyn has been a juried poet for the Houston Poetry Fest, a finalist in the National Poetry Series Open Competition, and a semifinalist for the Philip Levine Prize for Poetry. She is the founding poetry editor for *Angels Flight • literary west.* Sherilyn lives in Southern California where she referees for the Los Angeles Derby Dolls.

LAVONNE LEONG | *Heat*

"I wrote 'Heat' deep in the pandemic winter of 2020–2021. That whole period cast us all back on our internal resources, and it became very clear what we could do for ourselves, and what we had relied on others to give to us. One of the things that got me through that year was learning, slowly, how to cook some of the Asian foods that I'd relied on restaurants or my relatives to provide. The application of heat, and the process of cooking, also causes transformation—and that idea had special valence for me right then."

SOCIAL
>Instagram: @LavonneLeong
>LinkedIn: @Lavonne-Leong

LAVONNE LEONG was born and raised in Hawai'i and now writes, hikes, and parents two mixed-race daughters in the Canadian Gulf Islands. She has a doctorate in English literature from Oxford University and is a master's candidate in strategic foresight at the University of Houston.

SELINA LI BI | *Amah - Postcard from Manila*

SOCIAL
   https://selinalibi.com/
   Twitter: @selinalibi

SELINA LI BI's writing has appeared in *riksha: Asian American Creative Arts in Action*, *Cha: An Asian Literary Journal*, *Red Weather* literary magazine, and *Cricket*. She also writes fiction and nonfiction for the educational market. Her chapbook, *Displaced*, an exploration of her experience as a second-generation Asian American, is scheduled for publication in the spring of 2022. She lives in North Dakota and holds an MFA in Creative Writing from Minnesota State University Moorhead.

JOANNA MAILANI LIMA | *Call and Response - 41(st) Birthday Noodles*

SOCIAL
   Instagram: @joannamailani5

JOANNA MAILANI LIMA is a spiritual wayfinder, creative storyteller, and lifelong student of Polynesian dance. Her artistic, academic, and clinical work explores culturally diverse families, social justice, and the healing power of expressive arts. Her essay "Sacred Story

Stitching" appears in the anthology *(Her)oics: Women's Lived Experiences During the Coronavirus Pandemic.* Joanna lives on Kumeyaay land, also known as San Diego, California.

GRACE HWANG LYNCH | *Behind the Mask*

"I wrote this piece in January 2021, as we neared the one-year anniversary of the COVID-19 pandemic. Lunar New Year reminded me of the previous holiday, which was the last "normal" family event and the beginning of my own wrestling with wearing a face mask, considering both protecting myself from the virus and how I (an East Asian American woman) would be perceived in that racially charged environment. One of my hopes in writing this piece is that it would shed light on how easy it is for misinformation to creep into our lives and how we all have the potential for change."

SOCIAL
gracehwanglynch.com
Facebook: @gracehwanglynchwriter
Instagram: @gracehwanglynch
Twitter: @GraceHwangLynch
LinkedIn: @gracehwanglynch
Medium.com: @gracehwanglynch

GRACE HWANG LYNCH is a Taiwanese American journalist and essayist in the San Francisco Bay Area. Her reporting on Asian America can be found at PRI, NPR, and NBC. Her essays have been published by *Tin House, Catapult, Paste,* and more. The anthologies *Lavanderia: A Mixed Load of Women, Wash, and Word* and *Mamas and Papas: On the Sublime and Heartbreaking Art of Parenting* (both San Diego City Works Press) have included her work.

ARETHA MATT | *My Home*

"I am inspired to write—yet also humbled—by the memories of my upbringing on the Navajo reservation. My life can easily be described as beauty entrenched in despair. In a place often known for poverty and oppression, I developed strength, insight, motivation, and tolerance. It was never lacking in love and forgiveness."

ARETHA MATT identifies as Charcoal Streaked People (Division of the Red Running into Water Clan). She is born of the Towering House People. She is a citizen of the Navajo Nation. Aretha teaches academic writing at the University of New Mexico–Gallup. She writes poetry and short stories.

DW MCKINNEY | *peril + power*

"'peril + power' is an offering of respect to a former colleague who became (and still is) a good friend. It portrays how we navigated a shared workspace as Black and AAPI women, finding ways to support each other professionally and personally in a predominantly white space. The title is a nod to a slogan used in the 1960s by AAPI activists in support of the Black Panther Party."

SOCIAL
>
> dwmckinney.com
> Instagram: @thedwmckinney
> Twitter: @thedwmckinney

DW MCKINNEY is a Black American writer and interviewer. An editorial fellow with Shenandoah Literary and the Writers' Colony at Dairy Hollow, she pens 3 PANELS, a graphic novels review column for *CNMN Magazine*. Her work has received nominations for *Best*

American Essays, the Pushcart Prize, and Best of the Net, and is featured in *Chicken Soup for the Soul, Desert Companion, Los Angeles Review of Books, HelloGiggles*, and *JMWW Journal*, among others. She currently serves as the nonfiction columns editor for *Raising Mothers Literary Magazine*.

SARAH E. MCQUATE | *(un)Taming the Beast*

"This essay is my attempt to practice writing about what's going on in my head instead of what's happened to me. I often obsess over trying to make someone (read: white people) feel something ('Gasp! I can't believe someone said that to you!'). Sure, that's cathartic, but it also minimizes me as the protagonist of my story. It's more empowering to give my own thoughts and feelings room to breathe."

SOCIAL

    sarahmcquate.com
    Twitter @potassiumwhale
    LinkedIn: @sarah-mcquate

SARAH E. MCQUATE is a half-Black, half-white scientist turned science writer. Sarah has a PhD in biochemistry from the University of Colorado Boulder and a science writing certificate from the University of California, Santa Cruz. Sarah has science stories published in a variety of outlets, including *Nature* and *Science*. Now Sarah writes about research news from the University of Washington's College of Engineering and Information School. Sarah spends her free time reading, exploring the Pacific Northwest, and learning how to figure skate. Sarah is also working on telling her own story.

CLAIRE MEUSCHKE | *Mean Well*

SELECT TITLES
UPEND, Blacksburg, VA: Noemi Press, 2020.

SOCIAL
Instagram: @clairemeuschke
Twitter: @ClaireMeuschke

CLAIRE MEUSCHKE is the author of *Upend* (Noemi Press, 2020), which was longlisted for the PEN/Voelcker Award. She is an urban farmer in Oakland, California.

DONNA MISCOLTA | *Brown*

"'Brown' is from a larger piece called 'Can't You Talk, Girl?' in which I examine moments in my childhood when I felt silenced, as if who I was and what I had to say had no importance in the world, a feeling based on the way others perceived me as a brown girl, which affected how I saw myself. Writing about such moments frees me from that silence."

SELECT TITLES
Living Color: Angie Rubio Stories: Jaded Ibis Press, 2020.
Hola and Goodbye: Una Familia in Stories, Chapel Hill, NC: Blair Publishing, 2016.
When the de la Cruz Family Danced, Hong Kong: Signal 8 Press, 2011.
"Regeneration of the Tongue," *Epiphany: A Literary Journal*, Spring/Summer 2021.
"This is Not a Dialogue," *Museum of Americana*, vol. 24, Summer 2021.

SOCIAL
> donnamiscolta.com
> Facebook: @DonnaMiscoltaWriter
> Instagram: @misdonnacolta
> Twitter: @DonnaMiscolta

DONNA MISCOLTA's third book of fiction, *Living Color: Angie Rubio Stories*, was named to the 2020 Latino Books of the Year list by the Las Comadres and Friends National Latino Book Club. Her story collection *Hola and Goodbye*, winner of the Doris Bakwin Award for Writing by a Woman, won an Independent Publishers Award for Best Regional Fiction and an International Latino Book Award for Best Latino-Focused Fiction. She's also the author of the novel *When the de la Cruz Family Danced*, which poet Rick Barot called "intricate, tender, and elegantly written—a necessary novel for our times."

SANDY NAMGUNG | *Running While Asian*

"'Running While Asian' navigates what it's like running as an Asian American woman. Asians are underrepresented in the fitness industry, which reflects the deep historical erasure and invisibility Asians have experienced and continue to experience today. Meanwhile, the objectification of Asian women is normalized. This work hopes to contribute to a new narrative that recognizes, respects, and values the diversity of Asians and their full personhood."

SELECT TITLES
> "Dear Allies and Antiracists, Where Are You?" *Medium*, 9 February 2021.
> "Lessons from a Japanese Canadian, a White Lesbian, and a Black Reverend," *I Am Asian. 50 People. 50 Stories.*, Loretta

M. Cheung, Kevin Wang, et. al, editors: Asian & Loud LC, 2020, pp. 191–98.

SOCIAL

Instagram: @sandynamgung
LinkedIn: @sandynamgung

SANDY NAMGUNG (she/her) is a Korean American writer based on Duwamish territory (Seattle, Washington). Born in Seoul, South Korea, Sandy immigrated with her family to the United States when she was three years old. Her writing is based on her experiences navigating between two different cultures and defining for herself what it means to be "Asian enough" and "American enough." Sandy was selected to contribute to *I Am Asian. 50 People. 50 Stories*, an anthology of writers within the Asian diaspora sharing their unique experiences. She earned a bachelor's degree in political science from the University of Washington.

SHAINA A. NEZ | *Haz'ą - To My Daughter's Future Bullies*

"Nonfiction writing surrounded my daughter—I wanted to capture everything we did. I never wanted to write about COVID-19. The year was dreadful and was the opposite of prolific. But seeing my daughter color, her motions, it reminded me of 'Haz'a,' the space we are all taking, and to write it felt needed. I was grateful my daughter brought me back to writing and the intent I started with."

SELECT TITLES

"What You Can't Say during a Family Hearing," *Yellow Medicine Review*, Spring 2021.
"Diné Bizaad Meets Bilagaana Bizaad," *Yellow Medicine Review*, Spring 2021.

"Táchiinii Women," *Yellow Medicine Review*, Spring 2021.
"Diné Abecedarian," *Massachusetts Review*, vol. 61, no. 4, 2020.

SOCIAL

Facebook: @shania.nez
Instagram: @na_na_shai

SHAINA A. NEZ is a Diné mother, writer, and first-year doctoral student. She is Táchii'nii born for Áshįįhi. Nez received her MFA in Creative Writing from the Institute of American Indian Arts. Nez serves as a Project Manager at Diné College in Shiprock, New Mexico. Her work has appeared in *The Massachusetts Review, Tribal College Journal, Yellow Medicine Review, Chapter House Magazine,* and elsewhere. Nez is a member of Saad Bee Hózhǫ: Diné Writers' Collective, an alum from *Tin House Press,* Summer 2021, and a recipient of the 2021 Open Door Career Advancement Grants for BIPOC women writers.

JOAN OBRA | *A Language Lost*

"With the deaths of my father and three of my grandparents, most of my strongest links to Philippine culture have slipped away. These losses leave me in a continual state of nostalgia. I'm writing stories about my elders, using their languages, to tie myself to them. One day, these stories will be all that's left to remind me of who I am."

SOCIAL

joanobra.com
Facebook: @joan.obra.writer
Instagram: @joan_obra
LinkedIn: @joanobra
Clubhouse: @joan_obra

JOAN OBRA is a Filipina American coffee producer and writer. She's a partner in Rusty's Hawaiian—a coffee farm, mill, and roastery on Hawaiʻi Island called "one of the world's most celebrated farms" by the *New York Times*. Obra wrote "Coffee Processing: An Artisan's Perspective" for *Coffee: A Comprehensive Guide to the Bean, the Beverage, and the Industry* (Rowman & Littlefield, 2013). Before joining her family's coffee farm, Obra was an award-winning journalist covering food for the *Fresno Bee* in Fresno, California. She holds a master's degree from the UC Berkeley Graduate School of Journalism.

PREETI PARIKH | *Manifesto for the Dreamland*

"This essay began as an impulse to render the female body within patriarchal spaces. I found myself rebelling against the ideas of 'purity' and 'chasteness' that seem closely linked to 'female honor' in my homeland's cultural and historical imagination."

SOCIAL
>   preetiparikh.com
>   Facebook: @poetpreeti
>   Instagram: @poetpreeti
>   Twitter: @poetpreeti

PREETI PARIKH is an Indian American poet and essayist whose work can be found in *Kweli Journal, Literary Mama, Ruminate Magazine*, and other literary journals and anthologies. With a past educational background in medicine and an MFA from the Rainier Writing Workshop, she is currently working on a book-length collection of poems and lyric essays. Born and raised in India, Preeti now lives with her family in a multigenerational household in Ohio. Besides working as a freelancer, she continues to explore her interests in indigo dyeing, textile arts, and image-text work.

DEESHA PHILYAW | *Daddy's Girl - The Exam - Tell Us You're a Black Guy Who Only Dates White Girls Without Telling Us You Only Date White Girls*

SELECT TITLES
The Secret Lives of Church Ladies. Morgantown: West Virginia University Press, 2020.

SOCIAL
deeshaphilyaw.com
Facebook: @DeeshaPhilyawWriter
Instagram: @deeshaphilyaw
Twitter: @DeeshaPhilyaw
LinkedIn: @deesha-philyaw

DEESHA PHILYAW's debut short story collection, *The Secret Lives of Church Ladies*, won the 2021 PEN/Faulkner Award for Fiction, the 2020/2021 Story Prize, and the 2020 *LA Times* Book Prize: The Art Seidenbaum Award for First Fiction, and was a finalist for the 2020 National Book Award for Fiction. *The Secret Lives of Church Ladies* focuses on Black women, sex, and the Black church, and is being adapted for television by HBO Max, with Tessa Thompson executive producing. Deesha is also a Kimbilio Fiction Fellow.

LONDON PINKNEY | *The Question - Redbone*

SOCIAL
Instagram: @london.pinkney

LONDON PINKNEY is a writer. She is the co-founder and editor in chief of *The Ana*. Pinkney is a fiction MFA candidate at San Francisco State University. She is the 2019 recipient of the Joe Brainard

Fellowship and the 2020 recipient of the Marcus Second Year Graduate Student Scholarship. Her work can be read in various places, including *Mirage #5 / Period[ical]*, *Seen and Heard*, and *OmniVerse*.

SAARIKA RAO | *Misnomer - A Seat at the Table*

"I've struggled with my own cultural identity issues from a young age, dealing with racism while balancing and embracing two cultures. Writing and processing has allowed me to grow, heal, and continue to empower myself."

SOCIAL
> Instagram: @abcdtherapist
> LinkedIn: @saarika-rao

SAARIKA RAO is a South Asian American woman born and raised in New York City who currently resides in Southern California. She is a psychotherapist and often works with clients of color who are trying to find their identity. She is passionate about mental health advocacy and the importance of sharing our stories and perspectives with the world, especially as a woman of color.

BARBARA JANE REYES | *Track: "You're the One," by Fanny (1971)*

SELECT TITLES
> *Letters to a Young Brown Girl*, Rochester, NY: BOA Editions, Ltd., 2020.
> *Invocation to Daughters*, San Francisco, CA: City Lights Publishers, 2017.
> *To Love as Aswang*, San Francisco, CA: Philippine American Writers and Artists, Inc., 2015.

210

Reyes, *Diwata*, Rochester, NY: BOA Editions, Ltd., 2010.
Poeta en San Francisco, Tinfish Press, 2005.

SOCIAL

barbarajanereyes.com
Twitter: @bjanepr

BARBARA JANE REYES was born in Manila, Philippines, and raised in the San Francisco Bay Area. She is the author of numerous works, including *Letters to a Young Brown Girl*, *Poeta en San Francisco*, and *Diwata*. She has received various accolades for her work, such as the James Laughlin Award of the Academy of American Poets. An Andrew W. Mellon Foundation Fellow, she obtained her BA at Berkeley and her MFA at San Francisco State. Today, she is an adjunct professor at University of San Francisco's Yuchengco Philippine Studies Program, and lives with her husband in Oakland.

ROSHNI RIAR | *Balancing Act - By Blood*

"I grew up in a predominantly white town, burdened with shame which impeded my ability to connect with my identity as a woman (then girl) of color. I spent decades divorcing myself from all the things that I didn't realize made me, me. This essay acknowledges that little girl who felt utterly torn, not knowing that as an adult, I would find my way back to our culture through writing."

SOCIAL

Instagram: @arekayare
Twitter: @arekayare
LinkedIn: @roshni-riar

211

ROSHNI RIAR (she/her) is an emerging writer and creative writing BFA student at UBC Vancouver. Working primarily in poetry and creative nonfiction, she explores the relationships between culture, language, trauma, and identity as a Panjabi woman. Her poetry has appeared in *Room Magazine*, *CV2 Magazine*, and *Antigonish Review*, with forthcoming publications in *Parentheses Journal* and *Canthius*, respectively. She also is a poetry reader for *Non.Plus Lit* and a contest reader for *PRISM International*.

KAREN RIGBY | *Autobiography as a Panamanian Botanical Index - Lunar Geography - Origin*

SELECT TITLES
> *Chinoiserie*, Boise: Ahsahta Press, 2012.

SOCIAL
> karenrigby.com

KAREN RIGBY was born in the Republic of Panama. She is half Chinese and half Panamanian American. A National Endowment for the Arts Literature Fellow, she lives in Arizona.

RAHNA REIKO RIZZUTO | *Imperfect Mother*

"I lost my mother to Alzheimer's when I had barely become a mother myself. Understanding who she was, and how much I do not know or have gotten wrong, has been essential both to my personal growth and my creative imagination."

SELECT TITLES

Shadow Child, New York: Grand Central Publishing, 2018.
Hiroshima in the Morning, New York: Feminist Press, 2010.
Why She Left Us, New York: HarperCollins, 1999.
The NuyorAsian Anthology: Asian American Writings About New York City (Associate Editor). Philadelphia, PA: Temple University Press, 1999.

SOCIAL

rahnareikorizzuto.com
Facebook: @RahnaReikoRizzuto
Twitter: @r3reiko
Instagram: @reiko_writes

RAHNA REIKO RIZZUTO is mixed-race Japanese/Caucasian, born in Hawaiʻi and raised in a small "cow town" on the Big Island. Her novel about the Japanese American incarceration camps, *Why She Left Us*, won an American Book Award. She is also the author of the novel *Shadow Child*, and the memoir *Hiroshima in the Morning*, which was a finalist for the National Book Critics Circle Award, among other honors. Reiko teaches in the Goddard College MFA in Creative Writing program. She is a recipient of a US/Japan Creative Artist Fellowship, funded by the National Endowment for the Arts. She lives in Brooklyn.

ADRIENNE ROBILLARD | *Just Like*

"As much as I wanted to fit in growing up, I grew tired of being pigeonholed, weary of the constant game of being paired with those to whom I most often did not belong. I wrote this piece after discussing the Chinese dentist with my mom and realizing that this is only a small glimpse of the 'just like' experiences both of us have had. There are many more."

213

SELECT TITLES
> *The 'Ohana Grill Cookbook* with Dawn Sakamoto Paiva, New York: Ulysses Press, 2020.
> *Maps and Tapes,* Honolulu: Hali'a Aloha Series/Legacy Isle Publishing, 2022.

SOCIAL
> adriennerobillard.com
> Instagram: @adriennerobillard
> Twitter: @acrobillard

ADRIENNE ROBILLARD won a William Saroyan Award for the first short story she wrote in high school in Fresno. She earned her MFA in Creative Writing at Mills College in 2000 and participated in the Tin House Summer's Writer Workshop in 2017. Her essay, "Try Wait," was published in the March 2018 American issue of the zine *We'll Never Have Paris.* She wrote *The 'Ohana Grill Cookbook*, published by Ulysses Press in September 2020. When she isn't teaching college English, Robillard is working on a YA novel.

DALEELAH SALEH | *Ramadan*

"I am so grateful to my mother for establishing Ramadan rituals, for ensuring that my brother and I were surrounded by Arab culture, and that we always felt the Ramadan spirit, despite not living in a Muslim country. I feel lucky to have grown up celebrating a holiday that taught me to see everything through a lens of gratitude, even when it felt like the world was ending."

SELECT TITLES

"In Flux," *CTLR + B*, edited by Molly MacDermot and Girls Write Now, New York: Girls Write Now, Inc., 2019.

"The New National Anthem," *Generation F*, edited by Molly MacDermot and Girls Write Now, New York: Girls Write Now, Inc., 2018.

SOCIAL

LinkedIn: @daleelahsaleh

DALEELAH SALEH is a proud New Yorker and Egyptian American. She is a Posse Scholar at Middlebury College, where she serves as a writer and editor for *The Middlebury Campus*. As a film and media studies major, Daleelah is constantly exploring the intersections of various systems of oppression using multimedia storytelling. Through her writing and extracurricular work, she hopes to challenge dominant narratives by creating positive representation of and for people in her communities.

SHEI SANCHEZ | *Border Between*

"It's been more than ten years since this happened and somehow, this particular event of 'assumption-labeling' still sticks with me. Though our family immigrated over twenty years before this story, I felt the weight of his assumption on all the things we had done in our lives. It awakened a re-questioning of an individual's place in society and the invisible hierarchies that create these assumptions."

SELECT TITLES

"Elegy with Green Mangos," *Sepia Journal*, vol. 1, Winter 2021.

"Composition," *Sheila-Na-Gig online*, vol. 5.3, Spring 2021.

"Detachment," *Gyroscope Review*, vol. 21-2, Spring 2021.

"Leaving Home," *Indolent Books*, 12 February 2020.
"Proto," *Essentially Athens Ohio: A Celebration of Spoken Word and Fine Art*, edited by Kari Gunter-Seymour, independently published, 2019.

SOCIAL

 sheisheiwrites.wordpress.com
 Facebook: @shei.shine
 Instagram: @sheishimi

SHEI SANCHEZ is a Filipina American writer, photographer, and yoga teacher from Jersey City, New Jersey. Her pieces have appeared in *Sheila-Na-Gig online*, *Autumn Sky Poetry Daily*, *Gyroscope Review*, *Dissonance Magazine*, and other places. She lives on a farm in Appalachian Ohio with her partner.

MISTY-LYNN SANICO | *Not Safe for Work*

"Even after so many encounters, it still surprises me how casually people can disguise racism behind compliments and dismiss centuries of exploitation of native women for a laugh. To openly question their error or rebuff the privilege of their benevolence is seen as rude and somehow proof of my hidden savagery. So, I've learned to be savage with my words, wielding the colonizer's language. Writing is my superpower."

SOCIAL

 hawaiireads.com
 Facebook: @mistysanico
 Instagram: @mistysanico
 Twitter: @mistysanico

MISTY-LYNN SANICO is a writer and editor in Honolulu, Hawaiʻi. A native Hawaiian, Misty-Lynn is co-founder of Hawaiʻi Reads and associate editor of *The Hawaiʻi Review of Books*. She also works for *Bamboo Ridge Press*, an independent, literary, nonprofit publisher. Her work has appeared in various journals and magazines.

MISTY SHOCK RULE | *Korean Culture Camp*

"My essay was written in April 2021 in the wake of the Atlanta shootings of six Asian American women. I was angry about the ways I had been diminished, processing how I had been complicit, and committing to speaking out. My daughter Penny has buoyed and inspired me as I've seen how open she is to her identity. I believe in and will fight for a better future for her."

SELECT TITLES
"UW Undergrad's First Novel, Optioned for a Movie, Features Big Robots and Even Bigger Feelings," *University of Washington News* blog, 2021.
"Finding a Taste of My Identity," *Eater Seattle*, 2020.
"Bush Garden, Symbol of Changes in the Chinatown-International District, Looks to the Future," *International Examiner,* 2018.
" 'How Many of You Have Never Had a Teacher of Color?' " *ParentMap*, 2018.
"From UW to Yakima, Dulce Gutiérrez has been guided by love for her community," *University of Washington Magazine*, 2016.

SOCIAL
eatingtheave.com
Twitter: @minheeshock
LinkedIn: @mistyshock

MISTY SHOCK RULE (she/her) was adopted from South Korea as a baby and grew up in Port Orchard, Washington. Now she lives in Seattle with her daughter Penny and husband Chris. It wasn't until she was thirty-eight that she realized she wanted to be a writer, after working in tech and politics. Misty has written for local publications like the *International Examiner, Eater Seattle*, and the *University of Washington Magazine*, and she spends her days working for *University of Washington News*. Misty enjoys trivia, reading, watching movies, baking, and jogging.

SJ SINDU | *Mother*

SELECT TITLES
    Shakti, New York: HarperAlley, 2023.
    Dominant Genes, New York: Black Lawrence Press, 2022.
    Blue-Skinned Gods, New York: Soho Press, 2021.
    Marriage of a Thousand Lies, New York: Soho Press, 2017.
    I Once Met You But You Were Dead, Wyncote, PA: Split/Lip Press, 2016.

SOCIAL
    sjsindu.com
    Facebook: @sjsindu
    Twitter: @sjsindu
    Instagram: @sjsindu

SJ SINDU is a Tamil diaspora author of two novels. Her first, *Marriage of a Thousand Lies*, won the Publishing Triangle Edmund White Award and was a Stonewall Honor Book and a finalist for a Lambda Literary Award. Sindu's second novel, *Blue-Skinned Gods*, was published in November 2021. A 2013 Lambda Literary Fellow,

Sindu holds a PhD in English and creative writing from Florida State University and teaches at the University of Toronto Scarborough.

GABRIELLE SMITH | *Mocha*

"'Mocha' was written to convey the pride of a Black teen who grew up being a part of the 'less than 1 percent.' I wanted to create an appreciation prose that illustrates the highlights of being African American and speak to other Black teenage girls who may also be coping with the struggles of being a minority and feeling troubled about their race."

SOCIAL
　　　Instagram: @g_machelle22

GABRIELLE SMITH is a student at Punahou School in Honolulu, Hawaiʻi. In school she helps with the editing of student publication, also having some of her work featured. Having lived in Hawaiʻi for nearly a decade, most of her work strives to depict the life of a Black female growing up in Hawaiʻi. Gabrielle lives on Oʻahu with her mother, father, and younger sister. When she isn't pouring her heart into her writing, she's playing soccer, creating art, or studying for her next exam.

JEN SORIANO | *Along the Way*

"At first I struggled with my contribution since I'm nonbinary and don't identify as an essentialized woman. Then this moment came to mind: the first time I bonded with others based purely on our identity as femme-bodied people, which meant sharing both vulnerability to and agency against gendered violence. It's less a coming-of-age than

219

a coming-out-of-individualism moment, and one small example of power that can come from the margins."

SOCIAL
>jensoriano.net
>Instagram: @jensorianowrites
>Twitter: @LionsWrite

JEN SORIANO (she/they) is a Filipinx American writer whose work blurs the lines between nonfiction, surrealism, and poetry. Her chapbook, *Making the Tongue Dry*, was published by Arts by the People in 2019 and is now in its third edition. Jen is the recipient of the 2019 Penelope Niven Prize, the 2019 *Fugue* Prose Prize, and fellowships from Hugo House, Vermont Studio Center, and Jack Jones Literary Arts. She lives with her family in Seattle on unceded Duwamish land. She is the author of an essay collection about historical trauma and the neuroscience of healing, forthcoming from Amistad in 2023.

LIZA SPARKS | *Driving to Work, I Think, What If I Were a White Man?*

"I wrote this piece thinking about the inequities that exist in our society that have historically privileged the identities of white straight cisgender men. How can we bring more equality and equity to our world? I believe the first thing is to name that which exists, so we know what we're trying to change—what has to change. It's important to acknowledge what is in order to imagine what can be."

SOCIAL
>lizasparks.com
>Facebook: @lizathepoet
>Instagram: @sparksliza534
>Twitter: @lizathepoet

LIZA SPARKS (she/her) is an intersectional feminist, writer, poet, and creative. She is a brown-multiracial-pansexual woman living and working in Colorado. Liza currently edits for the online artist-centric news and media platform Dirt Media. Her work has appeared with *Repave Magazine*, *Bozalta Collective*, *Cosmonauts Avenue*, and many others, and is forthcoming with *Honey Literary* and *Split This Rock*.

ANUPAMA SPENCER | *Only Pinks, Please*

"Navigating life as a female is hard by itself. Add some color to it and life is doubly hard. Skin color has dictated many things in my life. One of them happens to be shopping. It might seem trivial, but shopping—the simple act of choosing clothes—has caused me trauma. I grew up thinking no color looks good against my brown skin. Dressing up and looking presentable became a challenging task, and there was considerable loss of confidence as a teen."

SOCIAL
Instagram: @bybookorbycook
Twitter: @mancmoody

ANUPAMA SPENCER (she/her) is an eLearning professional based in India. She began writing seriously after the pandemic hit. Her work has appeared in *The Minison Project* and *Flash Fiction Frontier*.

ELIZABETH SU | *Back to the Roots - Split in Half*

"As a third-generation, biracial Asian American, I feel terribly disconnected from my Chinese heritage. I never quite know where I fit in. Too white for the Asians, too Asian for the whites. I wrote these pieces to reclaim my racial identity and grapple with my feelings of 'not enough.' Sometimes we have to write ourselves into existence."

SOCIAL
>   elizabethsu.com
>   Facebook: @heyelizabethsu
>   Instagram: @heyelizabethsu
>   Twitter: @heyelizabethsu
>   LinkedIn: @elizabethsu

ELIZABETH SU is a mixed-race Asian American writer, perfectionism expert, and founder of a publication and network for women called Monday Vibes, named "12 Newsletters Actually Worth Opening" by Zoella. Following a decade in Silicon Valley, Elizabeth earned her master's degree in clinical psychology from Columbia University, where she studied burnout and perfectionism. She's written for and been featured in numerous media outlets, including *Talkspace, PopSugar, Create and Cultivate, Bustle, InHerSight,* and *Authority Magazine,* among others. Elizabeth is all about helping women learn to love themselves, imperfections and all. She's currently working on her first book around these topics.

VICTORIA SUN | *Meet the Minority*

"I had gone from growing up in Flushing, Queen's rich diversity to attending a small high school in Connecticut, where many of my peers had never interacted with an Asian American. This piece was written out of my frustration, to show that I was not exotic. I was a student looking for recognition that I could transcend the expectations of the stereotypes of an Asian woman."

SELECT TITLES

> *Fast Fierce Women*, edited by Gina Barreca, Norwalk, CT: Woodhall Press, 2022.
> *Connecticut Student Writers Project Volume XXXVII*, edited by Connecticut Writing Project, Storrs, 2015.

SOCIAL

> LinkedIn: @victoriasunwriter

VICTORIA SUN is a graduate of the University of Connecticut. She has won a national silver medal from the Scholastic Art and Writing Awards in the category of humor. In 2015, she became a published poet in the *Connecticut Student Writers Project Volume XXXVII*.

YONG TAKAHASHI | *Cafeteria Tree - Special Education*

"'Cafeteria Tree' and 'Special Education' are part of my upcoming poetic memoir. I was the first Asian student in a 1970s Midwestern community. My parents threw me into school hoping the American educational system would spit out a successful adult. Neither the students nor the teachers knew how to deal with me. Snapshots of my childhood show how I lived between a White and Yellow world."

SOCIAL

> yctwriter.com
> linktr.ee/yctwriter
> Instagram: @yctwriter
> Twitter: @yctwriter

YONG TAKAHASHI is the author of *The Escape to Candyland*. She was a finalist in The Restless Books Prize for New Immigrant Writing, Southern Fried Karma Novel Contest, *Gemini Magazine* Short Story

Contest, and Georgia Writers Association Flash Fiction Contest. She was awarded Best Pitch at the Atlanta Writers Club Conference.

GRACE TALUSAN | *Searching*

"Whether I am scanning the little boxes in a Zoom room or the booths in a diner, I still search. I want to know, *Am I welcome here? Am I safe?* I comfort myself with Toni Morrison's words, where she says that the function of racism is distraction—that 'it keeps you from doing your work. It keeps you explaining, over and over again, your reason for being.'"

SELECT TITLES
> *The Body Papers: A Memoir*, Brooklyn, NY: Restless Books, 2019.

SOCIAL
> gracetalusan.com
> Instagram: @gracetalusanwriter
> Twitter: @gracet09
> LinkedIn: @grace-talusan-writer

GRACE TALUSAN was born in the Philippines and raised in New England. She graduated from Tufts University and the MFA Program in Writing at UC Irvine. She is the recipient of a US Fulbright Fellowship to the Philippines and an Artist Fellowship Award from the Massachusetts Cultural Council. She taught writing for many years at Tufts University and Grub Street, and is currently the Fannie Hurst Writer-in-Residence at Brandeis University. Her memoir, *The Body Papers*, won the Massachusetts Book Award in nonfiction, the Restless Books Prize for New Immigrant Writing, and was a *New York Times* Editors' Choice selection.

JEANNE TANAKA | *Watch Out, There Might Be Spies in the Room*

"Growing up our neighbors and best friends were white, but race was never an issue. We weren't different, and we were just as 'American' as everybody else. That teacher's cruelty lit a fire within me. It inspired me to live a life of speaking out against discrimination and injustice because no person should experience the humiliation and pain that I did simply because of the color of their skin."

At the age of eighteen, JEANNE TANAKA was interned at Tule Lake Internment Camp and spent the next four years of her life behind its barbed-wire fence. She has been featured in the documentaries *Resistance at Tule Lake* and *Injustice at Home*, and has been interviewed for numerous publications. Jeanne, an ardent political and social activist and proud Gonzaga alumna, lives in Spokane, Washington. She is ninety-eight years old.

IMANI TOLLIVER | *these hands*

"As a descendant of Harriet Tubman, I know that our blood shares the same intention: an unwavering commitment to justice for our people, family, and all those we love. I am committed to the big work, taking the big chances, and telling the big truths. My voice, through poetry, creates a path of authenticity that I stand firmly upon every day. It anchors me. And for this, I am grateful."

SELECT TITLES

Runaway. Los Angeles: World Stage Press, 2017.
Voices from Leimert Redux, edited by Shonda Buchanan, Los Angeles: Harriet Tubman Press, 2017.
Corners of the Mouth: A Celebration of Thirty Years at the Annual San Luis Obispo Poetry Festival, edited by Kevin Patrick

Sullivan, Patti Sullivan, and Youssef Alaoui Fdili, Philadelphia, PA: Deer Tree Press, 2015.
Her Kind, A Literary Community Powered By Vida: Women in Literary Arts, Herkind.org, September 2013.
Don't Blame the Ugly Mug, Los Angeles: Moon Tide Press, 2011.

SOCIAL
imanitolliver.com
Facebook: @ImaniTolliverPoet, @imani.tolliver
Instagram: @imanitolliver
Twitter: @imanitolliver
LinkedIn: @imani-tolliver

IMANI TOLLIVER (she/her) is an award-winning Black lesbian poet, artist, educator, public speaker, and event producer. An interdisciplinary artist, she is a collagist and watercolorist. She is a graduate of Howard University, a Cave Canem Fellow, and served as poet laureate for the Watts Towers Arts Center. She has also been recognized by the City of Los Angeles for her work as a promoter, host, and publicist in support of the literary arts in Southern California.

FRANCES KAI-HWA WANG | *Auntie's House*

SELECT TITLES
Beyond Vincent Chin: Legacies in Activism and Art, Detroit, MI: Wayne State University Press, 2023.
You Cannot Resist Me When My Hair Is in Braids, Detroit, MI: Wayne State University Press, 2022.
Dreams of the Diaspora: Frances Kai-Hwa Wang Media, 2014.
Where the Lava Meets the Sea—Asian Pacific American Postcards from Hawai'i: Frances Kai-Hwa Wang Media, 2013.

Imaginary Affairs—Postcards from an Imagined Life: Frances Kai-Hwa Wang Media, 2012.

SOCIAL
franceskaihwawang.com
Facebook: @franceskaihwawang
Instagram: @franceskaihwawang
Twitter: @fkwang
LinkedIn: @franceskaihwawang

FRANCES KAI-HWA WANG is a poet, essayist, journalist, and activist focused on issues of Asian America, race, justice, and the arts. Her writing has appeared in *NBCAsianAmerica, PRIGlobalNation, Center for Asian American Media, Cha Asian Literary Journal, Kartika Review*, and *Drunken Boat*. She teaches Asian / Pacific Islander American Studies at University of Michigan and creative writing at University of Hawaiʻi Hilo. She authored three prose poetry chapbooks and *You Cannot Resist Me When My Hair Is in Braids* (Wayne State University Press, 2022). She co-created a multimedia artwork for Smithsonian Asian Pacific American Center and is a Knight Arts Challenge Detroit artist.

KEʻALOHI WANG | *Hapa*

"When I was young, I didn't understand why my grandma praised my European features. To me, she was beautiful and graceful, and I wanted to be like her. As I grew older, I began to understand the nuances of growing up in Hawaiʻi in the 1930s and 1940s as an Okinawan girl. In this piece, I wanted to honor the childhood my grandma lived and imagine how it shaped who she is today."

SOCIAL
Facebook: @kealohi.wang
Instagram: @fromalohi

KEʻALOHI WANG was born on the island of Oʻahu and raised on Hawaiʻi Island in the ahupuaʻa of Honokōhauiki. She gets both her Okinawan and Chinese heritage from her father and her English, Scots-Irish, and Bavarian heritage from her Tennessee mother. Keʻalohi was raised on the slopes of Hualālai with a mother who loved classic literature and a father who loved the ocean. Both of these influences are seen in her writing.

DURTHY A. WASHINGTON | *Mischling*

"As people of color living in the shadow of White Supremacy, we will always be called upon to claim our identities and create new names for ourselves. While I grew up amidst anti-German and anti-Black violence, my two Japanese American granddaughters—living in a time of virulent anti-Asian violence—at least have hafu role models like Naomi Osaka and Ariana Miyamoto. Still, I wonder how far we've really come."

SELECT TITLES
"Outsiders and Others: Revisiting Richard Wright's Underground Man," *Connections and Influences in the Russian and American Short Story*, edited by Jeff Birkenstein and Robert C. Hauhart. Lanham, MD: Lexington Books, 2021.
"Sonny's Blues," *Encyclopedia of the Black Arts Movement*, edited by Verner D. Mitchell, Lanham, MD: Rowman & Littlefield, 2019.

"Exploring the LIST Paradigm: Reading and Teaching Beloved,"
Critical Insights: Beloved, edited by Maureen N. Eke, Amenia,
NY: Grey House Publishing, 2015.

"Third World Girl as Superhero in Junot Díaz's *The Brief
Wondrous Life of Oscar Wao*," The Image of the Hero in
Literature, Media, and Society: Proceedings of the Society
for the Interdisciplinary Study of Social Imagery, Conference
at Colorado State University, June 2014.

Washington, Durthy, and Ernest J. Gaines, "Teaching Ernest
Gaines's *A Lesson Before Dying*," *Academic Exchange Quarterly*,
Summer 2008.

An Afro-German writer, seminar leader, and former English professor
who has taught in Russia, Japan, and the United States, DURTHY A.
WASHINGTON has published numerous articles and essays on the
works of African American authors, including James Baldwin, Richard Wright, Ralph Ellison, Ernest Gaines, and Toni Morrison. She is
the founder of LitUnlocked, which offers workshops and seminars
dedicated to the art of mindful, culturally responsive reading. Each
workshop centers on the LIST Paradigm, an innovative approach to
critical reading that helps readers *unlock* the power of literature with
four *keys to culture*: Language, Identity, Space, and Time.

ZINARIA WILLIAMS | *Instilled Confidence*

"Inspiration for this essay came from my writing teacher, David Mura,
who tasked me with looking at each stage of my life with a racial lens
and then being brave enough to put it on the page."

SOCIAL
    enduringcaduceus.com
    Instagram: @zwilliamsmd

ZINARIA WILLIAMS, is a board-certified ophthalmic plastic surgeon, writer, and Queens Arts Fund New Work Grant recipient. After decades of being published within ophthalmology textbooks and peer-reviewed journals, her writing shifted from scientific to narrative. She now focuses on themes illustrating the harmful consequences medical training can have on doctors, juxtaposed against the struggles of patients who suffer the downstream effects. Dr. Williams cares for patients at a public hospital in Queens, New York. She is currently completing a memoir recounting how she lost empathy for patients during a grueling yearlong internship and the steps she took to reclaim it.

JANE WONG | *Give Us Our Crowns - MAD*

"I wrote MAD thinking about anger and resistance via a Mad Libs form; it also pushes back against stereotypes of Asian women being silent and submissive."

SELECT TITLES
> *How to Not Be Afraid of Everything*, Farmington, ME: Alice James Books, 2021.
> *Overpour*, Notre Dame, IN: Action Books, 2016.

SOCIAL
> janewongwriter.com
> Facebook: @jane.wong.102
> Instagram: @paradeofcats

JANE WONG is the author of *How to Not Be Afraid of Everything* (Alice James, 2021) and *Overpour* (Action Books, 2016). Her debut memoir, *Meet Me Tonight in Atlantic City*, is forthcoming from

Tin House. Her poems and essays can be found in *Best American Nonrequired Reading 2019*, *Best American Poetry 2015*, *American Poetry Review*, *POETRY*, *Virginia Quarterly Review*, *McSweeney's*, and *Ecotone*. A Kundiman fellow, she is the recipient of a Pushcart Prize, fellowships and residencies from Harvard's Woodberry Poetry Room, the US Fulbright Program, Artist Trust, the Fine Arts Work Center, Bread Loaf, Hedgebrook, Willapa Bay, the Jentel Foundation, Mineral School, and others. She is an associate professor at Western Washington University.

INQUIRY AND RESPONSE:
SOME QUESTIONS TO CONSIDER

Consider the following questions as a pathway to richer discussions about the intersection of race and gender in America. We invite you to explore deeply and find yourself in these questions, and join the conversations started by the writers of these essays.

GENERAL CONNECTIONS
1. Which essay(s) do you resonate with the most? Why?
2. Which essay(s) feels most aligned with your own experiences? Which piece diverges the most?
3. Which essay(s) make you feel uncomfortable? Can you share why?
4. The book's title was taken from a poem by Lucille Clifton. How well does it work with the essays contained within? How do you feel about the term "nonwhite"?
5. What new ideas and/or questions surface for you as you read through this anthology?
6. Were any of the pieces surprising? How so?
7. Is there an essay you can't stop thinking about? What does it bring up for you? Are there one or two sentences in the essay that stay with you?

AUTHOR CRAFT / MICRO ESSAY FORM
8. What's your response to the micro essay form? How might this anthology feel different if the pieces had been longer?
9. How did these authors choose to tell their stories? What did you notice about the various storytelling styles? How does this compare to other personal narratives you've read?
10. Shaina Nez ("To My Daughter's Future Bullies") and Leena Jun ("Dear White Evangelicals") use the epistolary form for

233

their micro essays. What effect does reading this as a letter have on you as a reader? What is the writer able to say by using this form versus a more traditional narrative form?

11. In "Autobiography as a Panamanian Botanical Index," Karen Rigby uses footnotes as a storytelling device. What do you think about this craft choice?

12. Writing micro conveys a lot of information in a small amount of space, at times showing the reader a transformation from the first word to the last. How does Devi Laskar's "I Words" accomplish this?

13. Much like negative space in art, there are powerful storytelling gaps left in micro prose. Jane Wong intentionally makes use of these gaps in her piece "MAD." What effect does the "unsaid" have on you as a reader?

14. Liza Sparks writes "Driving to Work, I Think, What If I Were a White Man" entirely in questions, while Theresa Falk writes "In Answer to Your Questions as You Pass Our Family on the Street" as answers. What effect do each of these forms have on you as a reader? What do these two essays say about the sorts of questions faced by women of color in particular?

15. In the micro essay, "The Question," London Pinkney asks us one simple yet profound question that can be pondered like a Zen koan. Is it one that you can answer?

RELATIONSHIPS

16. In "Whose Skin Is My Skin?," Saheli Khastagir shares a story about family and self-perception. What thoughts does this piece evoke as you reflect about the role that family plays in identity formation?

17. SJ Sindu's "Mother" offers a chronology of a mother-daughter relationship, exploring what is both spoken and unspoken. How do your parents communicate their love or fears? How do you express your love or fears to the people closest to you?

18. Several of these essays reflect on identity and family through the lens of adoption. Mee Ok Icaro ("Real Mom") and Joanna Mailani Lima ("Call and Response") write about two different experiences with their adoptive parents. What thoughts/questions surface for you as you read these pieces?

19. How do friends support/detract from your sense of self—in particular, your identity as a woman of color?

20. As you read Theresa Falk's "To My Daughter Reading Tolkien," what thoughts surface for you about the role of storytelling in intergenerational relationships?

21. In Deesha Philyaw's "Daddy's Girl," her father announces that he has a new girlfriend and says, "Oh, but I got me a white girl." Discuss how this particular revelation might affect his daughter, and why.

CHILDHOOD MEMORIES/EXPERIENCES

22. We carry many experiences from our childhood, and some of those experiences are reflected in these pieces. What do you still carry, and how has that impacted who you are today?

23. In "Sugar Coated (1979)," Carla Crujido recounts a painful childhood memory. How might writing serve as a "response" to such experiences, thereby allowing us an opportunity to reclaim our strength by speaking back to those who have wronged us?

24. As you read through these micro essays, especially those recounting painful or traumatic experiences, what role do you feel writing can play in the healing process?

25. Specific objects are often strongly tied to childhood memories. In "Collector's Item," Alyssa Jocson Porter remembers a Filipina Barbie given to her by her mother. As you read her essay, what resonates with you? What objects evoke memories for you?

26. Food can be a source of comfort, but for others, it can be linked to pain. Think about the different role that food plays in Lavonne Leong's "Heat" and Daleelah Saleh's "Ramadan"

versus Yong Takahashi's "Cafeteria Tree" and Kaitlyn Hsu's "Lunch." What personal memories do you have that are linked to food? What stays with you no matter how much time has passed?

IMPACT OF SOCIETY ON SELF

27. As people of color, we can't help but be affected by societal events and how they may impact us both directly and indirectly based on the color of our skin. Grace Hwang Lynch ("Behind the Mask"), Julie Hakim Azzam ("How to Erase an Arab"), and Jeanne Tanaka ("Watch Out, There Might Be Spies in the Room") explore the intersection between current events and personal/family life. When have you been personally affected by societal or political events?

28. In "Beige Mask #2," Chelsea Hicks explores how society doesn't just impact our self-perceptions, it also affects our relationships with other people of color. What thoughts or questions does this piece raise for you?

29. In "Watch Out, There Might Be Spies in the Room," Jeanne Tanaka writes, "We had around three months while they built the camps to sell or get rid of everything we owned except for what we were able to carry." If you were forced to leave your home, what would you pack into a single suitcase to take with you into your new life?

30. In "Women in the Fracklands," Toni Jensen asks, "How many close calls constitute a violence?" How many times do we allow an act to occur before naming the danger avoided or inflicted?

LANGUAGE

31. In "these hands," Imani Tolliver remembers the painful words that were thrust upon her and how she reclaims them in a process of rebirth. What resonates with you from this essay?

236

32. What are the different "languages" we are called to speak as women of color? How do you speak at home versus the way you speak at work or in public? What barriers do you encounter with language—either the language of your birth, your cultural ethnicity, or the community in which you currently live?

33. In "Hues of Mama," Sabina Khan-Ibarra writes "Mama is a brilliant splash of pomegranate juice on white cloth." Tina Ehsanipour also uses the pomegranate as a symbol of strength in her essay, "Pomegranates," writing that "Pomegranates don't hide. We are meant to stain everything we touch." If you had to capture your own strength symbolically, how would you describe it?

SENSE OF BELONGING

34. In "Currents," Yi Shun Lai describes towns that are welcoming and unwelcoming, noting the way "the room chills . . . or goes quiet." What are ways you or others may have encountered, or offered, a similar response?

35. We sometimes find ourselves longing—for our homeland, for our ancestral tongue, for that feeling of belonging. As you read Joan Obra's "A Language Lost," what resonates with you about how she talks about her experience of being "left with pieces of conversations, always longing to belong?"

36. Both Alison Feuerwerker ("Eggs") and Amal Iman ("Hyper/in/visible") explore a desire to be seen. In what ways do you personally feel seen or unseen?

37. In "weightless," Anastacia-Reneé writes, "it's amazing what they expect from you." What expectations do we put on women of cultures not our own?

38. María Alejandra Barrios offers this first line in "The First Warm Day of the Year": "What does it mean to be an immigrant in a country that doesn't love you back?" How would you answer the question posed by Barrios?

39. In "Mean Well," Claire Meuschke writes, "It is difficult to identify as a target when I felt so unseen in the first place." Have you ever felt this way? How? Why?

40. In "Self-Portrait with No Flag," Safia Elhillo offers her reflections on how she has decided to pledge allegiance to her loved ones, rather than a country. How do you claim a place of belonging? Where do you pledge your allegiance?

PHYSICAL APPEARANCE

41. Physical appearance is a recurring theme in many of the essays. In "Only Pinks, Please," Anupama Spencer reflects on how she was only allowed to wear certain colored clothes as a child. Sarah McQuate's "(un)Taming the Beast" details the author's acceptance of her natural hair. How do you and the people around you express themselves through their clothing or hair?

42. In her essay, "In My Skin: An Autobiography," Fatimah Finney traces her experiences with her skin. What is powerful about the way she shares these reflections?

43. In both "A Tale I Have Never Lived" (Helena Garcia) and "Cindyjawea" (CMarie Fuhrman), the authors are told they cannot dress as Snow White because of the color of their skin. Fuhrman further explores the relationship between race and costumes in "Dress Up Like an Indian," in which she explains why dressing up like an Indian woman is harmful. In what ways can dressing up be a liberatory experience? In what ways can it be damaging or destructive?

44. Jane Wong's "Give Us Our Crowns" speaks of the seemingly impossible beauty standards in China and then asks, "How is this different from US beauty standards?" Is there a difference, and/or how are they the same?

45. In "Brown Baby," Kristiana Kahakauwila asks, "Is it pride to want to look who we are—as if who we are is in how we look?" Do you agree or disagree?

SELF-IDENTITY

46. Our identities evolve over time. In "On Being Made Whole," 'Iolani Brosio explores the role her ancestors played in making her who she is, while in "Korean Culture Camp," Misty Shock Rule shares how her cultural identity shifts because of her young daughter. What do these two essays make you think about your own cultural identity formation?

47. In Victoria K. Gonzales's essay, "Part of the Problem," the author grapples with speaking up while trying to keep the peace. Were there times when you had difficulty staying authentic to yourself and/or your cultural or ethnic identity? What did you give up in order to avoid conflict? If you could go back and make a different choice, what would it be?

48. In "exceptional," Anastacia-Reneé explores her identity in relation to people's expectations of her as a Black woman. What resonates with you about the piece?

49. Both Margarita Cruz ("Are You Sure That Isn't Your Drinking Name?") and Loralee Abercrombie ("Name") reflect on the way others perceive them based on their name. How would you describe your relationship to your name, and when has it been a challenge for you?

50. Being bicultural brings its own experiences and sentiments. In "Mischling," Durthy A. Washington writes, "And at last, I understand: my challenge was never about choosing sides, but about belonging to myself and being at home in my own skin." What resonates with you as you read this final line of her micro essay?

CRAFTING THE MICRO ESSAY
BY DARIEN HSU GEE

Writing micro may seem like a popular trend, but short forms have a long literary history. For centuries in China, there have been "pocket-size" stories, "palm-size" stories, and the ever-popular "smoke-long" stories, which are stories that can be read in the time it takes the reader to smoke a cigarette. Definitions and word count may vary, but the practice of writing—and reading—short is about true decision making, about tuning in deliberately and with great focus to what is wanting to be said or shared in a moment.

Flash, postcard, micro, vignette, snapshot, nano, tweets, and Six-Word Memoirs® challenge the idea that you need a lot of space to write or say something important. Writing in short is an opportunity to cut to the chase, to distill what is most essential into a few carefully considered words, to center a single experience or thought. At the same time, writers can cover a tremendous amount of ground—even whole lifetimes—in just a few sentences.

WHAT IS MICRO?

For *Nonwhite and Woman*, we define micro as 300 words or less, not including the title. The container of word count is a powerful way to not only help us organize our thoughts but pushes us to look at our words more bravely. This is not to say that longer essays don't serve a purpose—of course they do. Not everything can be written in micro—micro is a specific form that serves a specific narrative purpose. Deciding on the right form for your words is one of the most important elements of the writing process.

241

BENEFITS OF WRITING MICRO

- **Kinder to the writer:** It's an accessible writing experience that doesn't demand a tremendous amount of time or energy compared with a full-length essay or book. It's also easier to revise, rip apart, rebuild, reconsider.

- **Kinder to the reader:** Reading micro can be done in short bursts without having to commit to pages of backstory or context. Well-written micro can be deeply fulfilling to a reader and offer unexpected emotional or intellectual pivots, often in the very last sentence.

- **Micro is a beginning:** Some micro essays become poems; others become longer essays; some become novels or book-length memoirs.

- **Micro is information:** Writing micro helps the writer see what feels most urgent and important, a spark waiting to burst into flame. It can serve as a springboard into other ideas, inspiration, or related creative work.

- **Micro as a building block:** You can craft a book based on micro essays or micro chapters.

- **Micro as a tool in the writer's toolbox:** Mastering micro will make you a better writer regardless of what genre you write. Micro teaches you not only how to communicate an idea or moment succinctly but also trains you to identify what isn't useful in the piece, however beautiful or lyrical it may be. Micro helps you jettison what you don't need and hold fast to what you do.

USING CONTAINERS

Containers help frame our writing practice and/or provide a structure for the final piece. It's an organizing principle that helps your brain understand what it's working with—the objectives, the constraints. Deadlines serve a similar purpose. Establishing a clear framework instructs the brain to do what you want it to do, not the other way around.

There are three containers I use to help guide my writing: word count, time, and/or focus.

The container of word count

For micro, the maximum word count is 300 (250 is another popular micro max). This does not include the title, so consider trying your first sentence, or part of your first sentence, as the title. The last sentence might work, too. Choose titles that are either direct or can be interpreted on multiple levels. I often tell my students who are writing micro to let the title do some heavy lifting when it comes to storytelling and/or imparting necessary information.

While drafting your work you don't have to worry about meeting your word count—that's what revision is for. But to ensure that you don't end up with pages and pages of writing, the container of time will help keep you in check.

The container of time

A container of time is brain training, be it ten minutes or ninety. Fifteen minutes is a reliable sweet spot for early micro drafts, as it doesn't allow time for overthinking or obsessing. You set the timer and go.

Before you begin, tell yourself your goal is to find the heart of what it is you want to say or share, the raw and most essential intention of the piece. Tell yourself you ultimately will want to accomplish this in a polished 300-word essay. Tell yourself that you are going to give yourself fifteen minutes to get it down, and then go for it.

You are training yourself to understand how much you can write in a specific period of time, and building up muscle memory of what 300 words looks like on a page. The goal isn't to write a polished micro right out of the gate, but to *remind* your mind that this is where you are headed. Once your mind knows, it'll figure out the route to get you there.

The container of focus

This is also known as the container of intention. Are you working off a specific prompt? Is there a theme, a person, or a moment you are trying to amplify? What is the purpose of this micro essay and/or the larger body of work? What is bothering or intriguing you? Is there an image you keep seeing, a line of dialogue or voice you keep hearing, a sensation you keep feeling? Like the container of time, you want to state what your intention is before you begin, being as vague or specific as you want, and then let the writing take you wherever you go. For early drafts it's important to stay open—sometimes what we want to say doesn't always make itself known for a few drafts.

TITLES

Titles are one of the best parts of writing micro, and when used effectively can be essential in framing the work. Titles aren't included in the word count, which means you can use the title to set the stage for what's about to come.

A FEW MORE THOUGHTS

- In general, straightforward writing is always the best place to start, and sometimes the end result is more effective. Fold in the lyric during revision if your hand stops moving and you start over-contemplating.

- Trust the stories that emerge on the page. Don't judge yourself or the work, or whether it even fits into what you ultimately want to do. Treat everything as a jumping-off point, and stay open to the possibility that there's something in your words that wants your attention, even if you don't know what it is yet.

- Sometimes what isn't on the page can be just as powerful. What isn't being said or written? What's missing? Who's missing? What can the reader take from between the lines? Where is there a gap? What might be conveyed without you having to spell it out?

TRY IT: SOME EXERCISES

If you don't know where to begin or even what you want to write about, start with a prompt.

Prompts may seem overly simplistic, but they are a way in. Your subconscious knows where it wants to end up, but it's waiting for you to start the journey. In other words: get writing and see where it goes. Find prompts online or start with one below:

1. Write about your name.
2. What do you see when you look in the mirror?
3. Write about a grandparent; a great-grandparent.
4. Write about a time something changed in an instant.
5. Write about a birthday party.
6. Write about a food you ate growing up.

7. Write about money.
8. Write about a family trip.
9. Write about a breakup.
10. What's a phrase or saying you heard as a young child?
11. Write about what you know.
12. Write about what you don't know.
13. Write about school lunches.
14. Write about a pet.
15. Write about a family secret.
16. Write about a photograph. What's outside the frame? What can't we see? Who took the picture?
17. Write about cheating.
18. Write about a woman in your family.
19. Write about being afraid.
20. Write about the pandemic.
21. Write about inheritance.
22. Write about do-overs.
23. Write about being "the new kid."
24. What are some things that are lost in translation?
25. Write about the weather, particularly weather you don't like or find challenging. What/where/when comes to mind?
26. Write about a comfort object.
27. Write about a misunderstanding.
28. Write about something broken.
29. Write about endings.
30. Write about beginnings.

REVISE IT: A SHORTCUT

When you're ready to revise, I recommend my shortcut revision process inspired by the craft essay, "But Tell It Slant: From Poetry to Prose and Back Again," written by Judith Ortiz Cofer. [3] Many of my writing students consider this process literary magic because it enables you to arrive much faster at a clean, well-considered, shining piece of prose. You can do this process in thirty to forty minutes, generating three drafts in total. I generally recommend that you do not exceed forty-five minutes when doing this first "round" of revision.

Initial prose draft
Write your first draft in prose using one or more containers. Set your intention before you write, and then let it go once the timer begins. When you're done, title the piece and determine your word count. Underline or highlight any words, phrases, or sentences that feel interesting. It may be something you don't like—that's okay. Make a note and move on.

Rewrite as a poem
Next, take ten minutes to rewrite the piece as a poem. Use a timer to make sure you don't go over. If you finish early, go back and ask yourself if there is anything else you want to say. No one is going to see it, so don't get anxious or judgmental about your work—remind yourself this is just part of your writing practice. You don't need to follow your original prose piece verbatim—in fact, it's better if you don't. If you end up going in another direction, that's fine.

When you're finished rewriting it, give the poem a different title and figure out your word count (determining your word count with

---

[3] *Writing Creative Nonfiction: Instruction and Insights from the Teachers of the Associated Writing Program,* edited by Carolyn Forché and Philip Gerard (Blue Ash, OH: Writer's Digest Books, 2001).

each draft, even if it's a poem, is part of the brain training I spoke of earlier). Like before, underline or highlight any words, phrases, or sentences that feel important. Read the poem aloud. Look at everything you've marked in both pieces. Look at the titles. Ask yourself, what is wanting to be known here?

Rewrite again as prose
Now, put away the two pieces so you cannot see them. On a clean sheet of paper or blank screen, try to rewrite the piece as prose. Use your memory or recall, but don't look at the original writing. Time yourself for ten minutes and follow the same process as above. When you're done, add up the words, give the piece a title, then read it out loud. Mark up the piece with the words or phrases that resonate.

Now look at all three pieces. Which of the three do you prefer? Why?

Sometimes each of the three pieces will launch a separate trajectory of their own. If so, go with it! Figure out what they each want to be.

You'll most likely have some revision to do, but this process cuts your revision time dramatically because it goes beyond the old-school process of laboring over each word or sentence, and allows us to hold a space for the larger intention of the piece. This process invites you to keep reconsidering what is trying to show up on the page, and gives the writing three different chances to decide how it wants to appear. It will let you leapfrog through your revision work and arrive much sooner at the place where you hope to be.

SHARE IT

Once you have at least three to five polished micro essays, send them out! Many literary journals will accept up to three pieces at a time, and your lyric essays might present well as prose poetry. Even if you plan to use your micro pieces in a full-length book, having previously published credits will often be useful. Remember, too, that publication is not the only goal—creative nonfiction micro essays have a place in family histories and narratives, can be thoughtfully shared in a birthday card or as a gift, and make powerful spoken word pieces. They provide a break from longer book projects and can help inject immediacy and clarity into stories that have lost their way. The micro essay is powerful, a nuclear burst of prose that will stay with the reader, as well as the writer, for a long time.

READ MORE

In addition to the excellent published work of our contributors, we invite you to explore these nonfiction and creative nonfiction titles written and/or edited by women of color. This list is by no means comprehensive, but serves as a starting point, amplifying creators who are women of color who write about their own lived experiences and/or issues that impact the lives of women of color.

MEMOIR, PERSONAL ESSAYS, ANTHOLOGIES

Rabab Abdulhadi, Evelyn Asultany, and Nadine Naber (editors), *Arab and Arab American Feminisms: Gender, Violence, and Belonging*

Gloria E. Anzaldúa, *Borderlands/La Frontera: The New Mestiza*

Sarah M. Broom, *The Yellow House: A Memoir*

Austin Channing Brown, *I'm Still Here: Black Dignity in a World Made for Whiteness*

Thi Bui, *The Best We Could Do: An Illustrated Memoir*

Margaret Busby (editor), *New Daughters of Africa*

Rebecca Carroll, *Surviving the White Gaze*

Victoria Chang and Marilyn Chin (editors), *Asian American Poetry: The Next Generation*

Sandra Cisneros, *A House of My Own: Stories from My Life*

Jennine Capo Crucet, *My Time Among the Whites: Notes from an Unfinished Education*

Rosayra Pablo Cruz, *The Book of Rosy: A Mother's Story of Separation at the Border*

251

Firoozeh Dumas, *Funny in Farsi: A Memoir of Growing up Iranian in America*

Gloria Edem (editor), *Well-Read Black Girl: Finding Our Stories, Discovering Ourselves*

Roxane Gay, *Hunger*

Danielle Geller, *Dog Flowers*

Joy Harjo, *Crazy Brave: A Memoir*

Joy Harjo with Leanne Howe, Jennifer Elise Foerster, and contributing editors, *When the Light of the World Was Subdued, Our Songs Came Through: A Norton Anthology of Native Nations Poetry*

Daisy Hernández, *A Cup of Water Under My Bed: A Memoir*

Daisy Hernández, *Colonize This!: Young Women of Color on Today's Feminism (Live Girls)*

Maria Hinojosa, *Once I Was You: A Memoir of Love and Hate in a Torn America*

The Hmong American Writers' Circle, *How Do I Begin?: A Hmong American Literary Anthology*

Cathy Park Hong, *Minor Feelings: An Asian American Reckoning*

Quiara Alegría Hudes, *My Broken Language: A Memoir*

Shirley Hune and Gail M. Nomura (editors), *Our Voices, Our Histories: Asian American and Pacific Islander Women*

Kenya Hunt, *Girl Gurl Grrrl: On Womanhood and Belonging in the Age of Black Girl Magic*

Mira Jacob, *Good Talk: A Memoir in Conversations*

Randa Jarrar, *Love Is an Ex-Country*

Valarie Kaur, *See No Stranger: A Memoir and Manifesto of Revolutionary Love*

Patrisse Khan-Cullors and asha bandele, *When They Call You a Terrorist*

Maxine Hong Kingston, *The Woman Warrior*

Mary Paik Lee, *Quiet Odyssey: A Pioneer Korean Woman in America*

Valeria Luiselli, *Tell Me How It Ends: An Essay in 40 Questions*

T. Kira Madden, *Long Live the Tribe of Fatherless Girls*

Terese Marie Mailhot, *Heart Berries: A Memoir*

Melody Moezzi, *The Rumi Prescription: How an Ancient Mystic Poet Changed My Modern Manic Life*

Wayétu Moor, *The Dragons, the Giant, the Women: A Memoir*

Cherríe Moraga and Gloria Anzaldúa (editors), *This Bridge Called My Back, Fourth Edition: Writings by Radical Women of Color*

Aimee Nezhukumatathil, *World of Wonders: In Praise of Fireflies, Whale Sharks, and Other Astonishments*

Michelle Obama, *Becoming*

Nadia Owusu, *Aftershocks*

Claudia Rankine, *Citizen: An American Lyric*

Monica Sone, *Nisei Daughter*

Natasha Trethewey, *Memorial Drive: A Daughter's Memoir*

Patrice Vecchione and Alyssa Raymond (editors), *Ink Knows No Borders: Poems of the Immigrant and Refugee Experience*

Qian Julie Wang, *Beautiful Country*

253

Elissa Washuta, *White Magic*

Jade Snow Wong, *Fifth Chinese Daughter*

Michelle Zauner, *Crying in H Mart: A Memoir*

NONFICTION

Stacey Abrams, *Our Time Is Now: Power, Purpose, and the Fight for a Fair America*

Maile Arvin, *Possessing Polynesians: The Science of Settler Colonial Whiteness in Hawai'i and Oceania*

Gaiutra Bahadur, *Coolie Woman: The Odyssey of Indenture*

Cristina Beltran, *The Trouble with Unity: Latino Politics and the Creation of Identity*

Keisha N. Blain, *Set of the World on Fire: Black Nationalist Women and the Global Struggle for Freedom*

Grace Lee Boggs, *The Next American Revolution: Sustainable Activism for the Twenty-First Century*

Felicia Rose Chavez, *The Anti-Racist Writing Workshop: How to Decolonize the Creative Classroom*

Soraya Chemaly, *Rage Becomes Her: The Power of Women's Anger*

Edwidge Danticat, *Create Dangerously: The Immigrant Artist at Work*

Angela Y. Davis, *Women, Race, & Class*

Roxanne Dunbar-Ortiz, *An Indigenous Peoples' History of the United States*

Jennifer L. Eberhardt, *Biased: Uncovering the Hidden Prejudice that Shapes What We See, Think, and Do*

254

Reni Eddo-Lodge, *Why I'm No Longer Talking to White People About Race*

Lynn Fujiwara, *Asian American Feminisms and Women of Color Politics (Decolonizing Feminism)*

Alicia Garza, *The Purpose of Power: How We Come Together When We Fall Apart*

Laura E. Gómez, *Inventing Latinos: A New Story of American Racism*

Ruby Hamad, *White Tears / Brown Scars: How White Feminism Betrays Women of Color*

Deepa Iyer, *We Too Sing America: South Asian, Arab, Muslim, and Sikh Immigrants Shape Our Multiracial Future*

Morgan Jerkins, *This Will Be My Undoing: Living at the Intersection of Black, Female, and Feminist in (White) America*

Mikki Kendall, *Hood Feminism: Notes from the Women that a Movement Forgot*

Erika Lee, *The Making of Asian America: A History*

Audre Lorde, *Sister Outsider: Essays and Speeches*

Dawn Bohulano Mabalon, *Little Manila Is in the Heart: The Making of the Filipina/o American Community in Stockton, California*

Neda Maghbouleh, *The Limits of Whiteness: Iranian Americans and the Everyday Politics of Race*

Patricia Preciado Martin, *Songs My Mother Sang to Me: An Oral History of Mexican American Women*

Brandy Nālani McDougall, *Finding Meaning: Kaona and Contemporary Hawaiian Literature*

255

Heather McGhee, *The Sum of Us: What Racism Costs Everyone and How We Can Prosper Together*

Lara Medina and Martha R. Gonzales (editors), *Voices from the Ancestors: Xicanx and Latinx Spiritual Expressions and Healing Practices*

G. Cristina Mora, *Making Hispanics: How Activists, Bureaucrats, and Media Constructed a New American*

Paisley Rekdal, *Appropriate: A Provocation*

Vicki L. Ruiz, *Cannery Women, Cannery Lives: Mexican Women, Unionization, and the California Food Processing Industry, 1930–1950*

Beverly Daniel Tatum, *Why Are All the Black Kids Sitting Together in the Cafeteria?: And Other Conversations About Race*

Dr. Haunani-Kay Trask, *From a Native Daughter: Colonialism and Sovereignty in Hawai'i*

Karla Cornejo Villavicencio, *The Undocumented Americans*

Jesmyn Ward (editor), *The Fire This Time: A New Generation Speaks about Race*

Isabel Wilkerson, *Caste: The Origins of Our Discontents*

Helen Zia, *Asian American Dreams: The Emergence of an American People*

PERMISSIONS

–

All other quotations and brief excerpts are used under Section 107 of the Copyright Revision Act of 1976. Further reuse may require permission from the copyright holder(s).

ACKNOWLEDGMENTS

From the NWW Editorial Team: In an effort to give authors complete ownership of their language and self-expression, we chose not to enforce a set of stylistic rules across the essays. Where possible, we deferred to the author's personal preference for spelling, italicization, diacritical marks, and/or treatment of English and non-English words. For all the stories we were able to include, we acknowledge there are many more waiting to find their voice in the world—may this book be one of many that gathers our stories together. Grateful acknowledgment is made to the publishing and creative team at Woodhall Press, in particular, David LeGere, who championed this book from its inception. Our heartfelt thanks to the authors who generously shared their work, as well as the many friends and colleagues who provided advice and guidance. Thank you.

From Darien: A huge thanks to my family, who have been with me through every draft of every book—Darrin, Maya, Eric, and Luke. Acknowledgment and appreciation to the women in my family who have shared their stories with me, and to the wonderful editorial team for this anthology--Carla, Amy, Daleelah, and Tina—who were steadfast companions on this journey.

From Carla: Mahalo to my son, Kai Crujido Pendell, for twenty-five years of inspiration. Everything I do, I do for you. A lifetime of thanks to my mother, Deanna Crujido, for teaching me, at a very early age, about the transformative nature of books. I love you both more than words can express. Thank you to Darien for asking me to join her on this literary adventure.

From Amy: My sincerest thanks to the Rice University English department, particularly Dr. Kirsten Ostherr and Dr. José Aranda, for the opportunity to work on this anthology through the Clancy

Taylor Summer Public Humanities Fund. Thank you to Darien for your invaluable mentorship throughout this journey. Much love and thanks to my parents for supporting me in all my endeavors.

From Daleelah: I'm infinitely grateful for all the amazing women in my life who inspire me and push me to grow, particularly my mother, Shireen, grandmother, Awatif, and aunt, Niveen. Thank you for loving me so fiercely. I also owe gratitude to the Sadie Nash Leadership Project and Girls Write Now, for helping me harness the power of my words. I am especially grateful for my writing mentor, Livia Nelson. Thanks for being the older sister I always wished for. And thanks to the sisters I chose for myself: Gabi, Shanizea, and Nadia. Lastly, I'm grateful to Darien for this incredible opportunity.

From Tina: Much love to my family—especially my parents and grandparents who gave me roots, my sisters who grew alongside me, and my husband Asaf and children Nadav and Shireen, for branching me in new directions. A big thank-you to my always encouraging agent Serene, who first told me about this anthology. And to Darien, thank you for the opportunity to work on this editorial team.

ABOUT THE NWW EDITORIAL TEAM

DARIEN HSU GEE is the author of five novels that have been translated into eleven languages. Her collection of micro memoirs, *Allegiance,* won the 2021 IPPY bronze award in the essays category. She is the winner of a 2019 Poetry Society of America Chapbook Fellowship Award for *Other Small Histories* and a 2015 Hawaiʻi Book Publishers' Ka Palapala Poʻokela Award of Excellence for *Writing the Hawaiʻi Memoir.* Darien is series editor and co-founder of the memoir writing and hybrid publishing program, Haliʻa Aloha. She lives with her family on the Island of Hawaiʻi.

CARLA CRUJIDO is a hapa writer of Filipino, Mexican, Norwegian, and German descent. Her work has appeared in *The Ana*, *Yellow Medicine Review*, *Ricepaper Magazine*, and elsewhere. Carla is a graduate of the MFA program at the Institute of American Indian Arts. Originally from San Francisco, she now calls Portland home.

AMY BOWER is a PhD student in English at Rice University where she studies nineteenth-century transatlantic Gothic literature. She is a Civic Humanist Lecturing Fellow and a recipient of the Clancy Taylor Summer Public Humanities Fund. When she is not reading or writing about literature, she is creating stories of her own. She is currently working on a novel that combines her love of history, fairy tales, and Gothic horror.

DALEELAH SALEH is a proud New Yorker and Egyptian American. She is a Posse Scholar at Middlebury College where she serves as a writer and editor for *The Middlebury Campus*. As a film and media studies major, she is constantly exploring the intersections of various systems of oppression using multimedia storytelling. Through her writing and extracurricular work, she hopes to challenge dominant narratives by creating positive representation of and for people in her communities.

TINA EHSANIPOUR is an Iranian-born, California-raised writer and high school English teacher. Her work has appeared in various places, including *Nowruz Journal, South Writ Large Magazine, In Short–The Podcast*, and *Five Minute Lit*, as well as onstage with Golden Thread Productions. Never outgrowing her childhood obsession with the magical, she enjoys writing fiction with a touch of magic.